Tell Me a Story, Grandma

Stories Connecting
Six Generations in My Family

Judith Delaney

DORRANCE
PUBLISHING CO
EST. 1920
PITTSBURGH, PENNSYLVANIA 15238

Dorrance Publishing Co
585 Alpha Drive
Pittsburgh, PA 15238
Visit our website at *www.dorrancebookstore.com*

ISBN: 978-1-6853-7056-5
eISBN: 978-1-6853-7903-2

Tell Me a Story, Grandma

Judith Delaney

To the memory of my dad, Hugh Thompson,
My storyteller,
The one who loved me loyally from my birth
Until his final breath,
The one who inspired me to be a storyteller.

Preface

The beginning of the year 2020 would bring a change. The life we all were accustomed to, life before COVID-19, would disappear. Our new life would be wearing masks, washing our hands, and social distancing. In the U.S. alone, nearly 380,000 lives would be lost that year due to the pandemic. The death toll would be especially high in the elderly. Many of these would be great-grandparents who had lived during times unknown to the younger generations. Their stories are important.

On April 30, 2020, a baby boy was born in Atlanta, Georgia. Bennie will hear stories I tell him. I'm his great-grandmother. I'll tell him stories about his mother, his grandfather, myself, my father, and my grandmother. I am the link to his heritage. Sadly, many babies born in 2020 will not have the opportunity to hear such stories. It is my hope this book will provide some insight to young adults and children deprived of their heritage by COVID-19.

A Letter to Bree and Jake

This book has been prepared as a wedding gift for you. I couldn't think of anything better to give you than your heritage. When you were a little girl, Bree, you, and your sisters liked for me to make up bedtime stories when you spent the night. Those memories are precious to me. My own grandmother, Grandma Iris, did the same in my childhood for my siblings, my cousins, and myself.

This book is a compilation of my writings over the years. Of course, most of it was done when I was a student at Prince George's Community College, where I took courses in paralegal, psychology, criminal justice, and literature. I was a regular contributor for the college's newspaper, *The Owl*, so some articles are included. I also wrote a monthly article for a bilingual newspaper when I lived in Mexico and have put a little of that in the book.

You will notice, Bree, that in some essays, my professors have made notes. I am including this in its original form because you are a teacher, and I thought you might enjoy seeing those notes. I regret that some writings are undated, but I have done my best to arrange them in chronological order.

You will also see that not everyone in the family is represented. My decision here is not to slight anyone, as I love everyone in the family the same; but rather, to just include what I think you might enjoy. I have other writings, and intend to continue writing, but it is my wish that you and Jake enjoy what I have selected. I love you both very much and wish you a forever of happiness in your marriage.

Table of Contents

1
My Story

My parents and grandparents, and their parents for as far back as our family research can establish, were country people. From family stories and a bit of knowledge about surnames, I have concluded that many in my family have genealogical connections to Ireland and England.

I can't say that any of my ancestors arrived with the Pilgrims or were ever addressed as "Lord" or "Lady," but I wouldn't be surprised if distinguished people exist in my lineage, as noble qualities certainly exist in my memory of many family members, both living and some now deceased. I believe I came from good stock, that my people had a "pioneer" spirit, and that they were intelligent, achievers, moralistic, and kind. I feel that way about myself and consider myself blessed, as I, and others, see it also in my children and grandchildren.

My father, Harold H. Thompson, the third of five boys, was born in 1922 in Barbour County, West Virginia. His father, Otis, was a farmer and coal miner. I remember him well. He had a fear of weather disasters and consequently had a compulsion to dig sub-basements under the house as storm cellars. On Saturday mornings, he went into town to buy groceries for the week. When he returned home, if you were a grandchild who happened to be in the house, you had the opportunity to sit on his lap and give him a kiss on the cheek in exchange for a banana. I was one child who tolerated the scratchy beard to get the treat.

My father's mother, Iris, became a mother figure to me. Since most of my cousins lived nearby, she frequently babysat us. She adored her grandchildren and spoiled us. Discipline was not a part of her character, but she did give us repeated warnings to be careful so as not to get hurt while playing, not to hurt one another, and to make up quickly if a disagreement arose. This may have stemmed from her experience of losing two siblings in accidents. She came from a musical family and sang at public events as a young woman. Three of her sons, my father included, formed a band, and played at what were then called "beer joints," local establishments where dancing to live country music was the weekend recreation. Of course, their wives accompanied them, so Grandma had the children for the night. She told us bedtime stories after lights out while we laid crosswise on her bed, which was the only way to fit all of us in the same bed. My grandfather had his own room in another section of the house, so our special time with her never interrupted his sleep. She sang ballads to us and loved to have her hair curled and brushed by her granddaughters. She also told each of us that we were her favorite grandchild and promised each of us the same picture of a collie and a little girl which hung over her bed. Where that picture is now, I do not know, but a picture of Grandma will live forever in my heart.

My maternal grandparents also had a strong influence on me. They were good people. They were especially proud of their 14 children, which included two sets of twins. They left behind well over 150 natural-born offspring at my grandmother's death.

The Corleys, to this day, faithfully hold their family reunion on July 4th each year.

My father was a soldier in the Italian Campaign of World War II and returned to America with post-traumatic stress disorder, which he treated with alcohol. My father was able to overcome his addiction a few years ago, but now is in the advanced stages of prostate cancer. He and I have a healthy relationship, and I will miss him terribly. He is my hero; not because he was finally able to break free of alcohol, but because he takes responsibility for his life choices. I never bonded with my mother.

I was born in the fall of 1947 and was unable to speak clearly enough for anyone to understand me except my older sister, who translated for me at the one-room schoolhouse I attended until the fifth grade. I enjoyed school and learning. Achieving good grades was a form of escape for me from the sadness of my environment at home.

I was very competitive. My older sister easily qualified for a special West Virginia award granted to the top four county students on a 200-question test relating to state history, government, and geography. When I entered eighth grade and it was my turn to prepare for the "Golden Horseshoe" contest, I found it necessary to apply myself studiously for months prior to the test. I also won, as did my younger sister, but learning was not easy for me. As an adult, I would later be diagnosed with ADD, a challenge quite a few other family members have dealt with.

During my senior year in high school, I participated in the Civil Service exam given to graduating members of the business curriculum. I left West Virginia for the "bright lights" of the big city, Washington, DC, in the summer of 1965. I was married that fall and became a mother the next year.

After working for several years for the federal government, I entered the legal secretary field, where I was exposed to corporate, trademark, and general practice law. As a long-time student of the Bible, the law of our land appealed to me as the laws given to the Nation of Israel always had. In the seventies, I left the downtown law firms to be closer to my two young children. Our daughter, Jodi, is now 33 and expecting her first child, while our son, Jason, is 30 and has three wonderful daughters.

I became secretary to Robert S. Slaby, a former real estate sales agent, who attended law school at night to realize his dream of having a small real estate law firm. Bob's specialty was real estate settlements, and I assisted him in his practice of general law while another secretary did the settlement work. His partner, Leo Green, the former mayor of the City of Bowie, practiced general law and became a State Senator. I did Mr. Green's secretarial work also.

In the late seventies, my husband and I were expecting our third child, and we felt it would be good for me to be a "stay-at-home mom." We sold our home in Bowie and embarked on a wonderful adventure to live in the country near Gettysburg, Pennsylvania, where several of my husband's co-workers lived, providing him with a carpool arrangement for the one and one-half hour commute to work in Rockville, Maryland.

Sadly, our baby boy died the day he was born. I became a real estate sales agent. A few years later, we returned to Bowie, Maryland, where I again became employed by Bob Slaby, who had now become a business office park developer. He had developed, contracted the construction of, and sold units of the Bowie Office Park Condominium at the intersection of Routes 450 and 197. He also built a one-story office building in front of the office park and leased the road frontage to McDonalds.Bob and I decided that I would be an independent contractor in my position as administrative assistant to him and the office park manager. I really enjoyed being in control of my time and working in an independent manner.

I later entered a new field of consulting. I became an "image consultant." I attended courses and became skilled in analyzing a person's complexion, hair, and eye color to determine which ranges of colors, shades, and tones best enhanced their look and gave them shopping guides to coordinate their wardrobe, as well as make-up for women. It was exciting for me. I began giving lectures on the subject, doing personal wardrobe analyses, and shopping for my clients. I represented a make-up line and three clothing lines. I had my own studio, worked in the client's home, and did group workshops. I frequently worked with local department and dress stores in presenting fashion and wardrobe seminars. One associate and I organized, marketed, and presented a major presentation at a local Sheraton Hotel meeting room attended by 200 individuals, where our guest speaker was an author of a popular wardrobe coordination guidebook. My daughter, Jodi, was a high school student at the time, and she frequently worked with me as my assistant and model.

In 1986, I was able to begin my present primary career, which I never plan to retire from. I am, as one of Jehovah's Witnesses, an ordained minister. My volunteer work to which I devote nearly 20 hours each week consists of calling on householders to present the good news of God's kingdom (a government which will soon rule the earth and eliminate the pain and suffering experienced by mankind since the fall of Adam in the Garden of Eden). Approximately half of the time I spend is in conducting personal one-on-one, 19-week Bible study courses. I attend five hours per week of instructional meetings to keep my skills sharp for this very important service to the community.

In 1991, my husband resigned from his full-time job to work alongside me in the ministry. Having raised our children, we sold our house, downsized our life, and opened an exterior cleaning business to support ourselves by working seasonally and part-time. My husband, Basil, also serves as an elder (joined by a body of other qualified men) in the various congregations to which we were sent as "trouble-shooters" to care for needs in the congregation. Our first assignment was in the inner-city of Washington, where drugs and violence were the routine. It was not unusual to hear gunshots where we lived and served. Our friends told us not to worry unless we heard a return fire or sirens. We were cautioned that the two of us should not walk on the streets without our companions unless we displayed our Bibles and Watchtower magazines, as our light-colored skin and business attire might be mistaken for law enforcement or child welfare agents, which could alienate us from those in the community. We had no such problems and thoroughly enjoyed our relationship with our spiritual brothers and sisters, who called us "the cream in their coffee."

Our secular part-time work in the exterior cleaning business consisted of using special equipment to create high pressure hot water capable of removing atmospheric dirt and pollution from the exterior of anything capable of withstanding water. Our equipment operated at 3000 PSI and heated the water to just below the boiling point. It was set up in a work van, and our business was called "All Kleen, Inc." We were incorporated in the State of Maryland and performed work throughout the metropolitan area.

Our first major job was to clean a limestone and brick mansion on Kalorama Road, NW, Washington, which was the residence of the French Ambassador. We rented an 80-foot bucket lift to get Basil to the top of the very steep roof of the three-story house to clean air pollution which had accumulated over a 90-year period since its construction. We positioned this monstrous machine on the back lawn of the $13 million property where the Ambassador hosted parties for internationally famous people. We were horrified when, after a drenching rain, the machine sank deep into the beautiful grass and refused to move. The Ambassador spent the entire month of July in France each year, so we had time before his return to solve this logistic problem and complete the project. Besides ourselves, we had two other workers on the crew. The lawn was repaired, and we earned our $16,000 fee.

We went on to clean two 12-story office buildings in Washington, and we obtained a three-year contract to wash a fleet of approximately 120 trucks, cars, and pieces of equipment for the electric company in Frederick, Maryland. We also cleaned sidewalks for 27 K-Mart stores in Maryland and Virginia. Sadly, due to health problems, we had to give up the business and start working for someone else in 1995.

After that, Basil and I became resident managers of a self-storage company in Bladensburg, Maryland, called U-Store Self Storage. Once again, due to health problems, I quit working but continued my ministerial activities. Basil remained on the job, and I am now pursuing a paralegal degree at Prince George's Community College.

(This autobiography was written in 1999 to complete an experiential learning class at Prince George's Community College.)

Chronological Table of Experience

Year	Professional Educational	Community
1947	Born	Philippi, WV
1957	My uncle was my teacher, began attending meetings of Jehovah's Witnesses. Led the class one day in his absence.	
1961	Entered high school. Attended convention of Jehovah's Witnesses.	Griffin Stadium, Washington, DC
1964	Worked after school at local hospital. Started dating future husband	
1965	Graduated with Honors. Started working as stenographer, moving up to legal secretary. Married Basil R. Delaney, 11/20.	
1966	Jodi Lynne born 11/23; 6 lbs., 12 oz.	
1970	Jason Roy born 8/13; 6 lbs., 4 oz	
1977	Began real estate sales. Took my father into our household, he was sober; we bonded. Read everything printed about alcoholism; attended AA and Ala-Non meetings	

	Jeremy Richard born 9/27; 8 lbs., 7 oz. Died 9/27.	
1980	Became administrative assistant.	
1982	Opened Judy Delaney & Associates; trained in color analysis. Went to "college of hard knocks" learning about ADHD; attended seminars at PGCC on ADHD	
1986	Had my fourth and final miscarriage. Became a full-time minister.	
1991	Purchased All Kleen, Inc.	
1992	Was one of three women qualified to travel with a crew of 100 skilled carpenters to Homestead, FL, to replace roofs of homes of Jehovah's Witness after Hurricane Andrew.	
	Brianna Rachelle born 11/13; 8 lb. 4 oz.	
1994	Kaitlin Elise born 1/4; 7 lb., 10 oz.	
1995	Began working at U-Store	
1998	Earned "A" in intercession, criminal law.	
1999	Discovered I had ADD.	

Self-Concept in the Dysfunctional Family

Judith L. Delaney
Speech 101H, Fall 2001
December 7, 2001

When my daughter, Jodi, was a small child, she came to me one day and announced that her brain talked to her. How I explained that phenomenon to my preschooler has long ago escaped my memory, but I'll never forget how cute it was that, upon discovering this wonderful new plaything, she used it so adeptly. Combined with a vivid imagination, that talking brain was always up to something. It told her marvelous stories, sometimes in the forms of dreams, other times fantasy. Of course, she no longer misbehaved. Now it was, "I did not want to do it, but my brain told me to!"

Self-talk begins in infancy. Children raised in dysfunctional families develop an immense structure of family proverbs which, although never spoken about, become the undeniable controlling force in establishing the resulting maladaptive behavior that sets some of these children up for clinical depression in adulthood.

I had the misfortune of being born into such a family. I have suffered the compounded pain of not only a dysfunctional family of origin, but also the genetic predisposition to chemical brain dysfunction resulting in the psychiatric diagnosis of major depression. Although my childhood was not easy, I survived it with a minimal number of bad choices. I had three big things going for me in adulthood: (1) I was able to develop a relationship with my Creator in my early twenties; (2) I married an emotionally stable and supportive husband who joined me in my faith; and (3) I was blessed with two wonderful and loving children.

Communicating, 8th Edition states: "We all engage in self-talk—a nearly constant subconscious monologue or inner speech with ourselves. Sometimes we are conscious of our vocalizing aloud within our heads, but self-talk is often silent speaking ... Even though it may be quiet, its impact can be enormous." (68) On the same page, *Communicating* quotes from an article published in *USAir Magazine* entitled "Talk Yourself Up" as follows: "We have a choice each time we think, to think positively or negatively ... that absolutely is our choice. Once we understand that our private thoughts are ours alone to determine, we can select to program our brains with empowering, confidence-building thoughts."

I am hopeful that by my identifying, discussing, and illustrating four of the most hideous, unspoken, but devastating, family proverbs adopted by myself and most other children of dysfunction, my readers will be assisted in their own efforts to recognize and defeat negative and destructive self-talk when it stems from the life-long patterns of a dysfunctional family environment.The first and often most negative family proverb of children in dysfunctional families is "I'm not important." Although I was never physically or sexually abused, I was unnurtured and neglected as a child. I do not recall being hugged, praised, or communicated with (other than what was necessary such as the assignment of chores, etc.). I do not recall my parents interacting positively with my siblings either, except those rare occasions when the infant in the family captured a semblance of affection. I was second in a family of eight children. My father affectionately teased us in a good-natured manner. I didn't feel I mattered. This negative self-talk can best be illustrated by imagining that you are in a room with several television screens. Each screen has the face of one of your parents or siblings, but no matter how much you try to communicate with any person on the screen, no one answers you. A neglected child forms the obvious conclusion that he or she, by being unnoticed, is also unimportant. This negative self-talk is, of course, untrue. Being neglected by your family does not diminish your true value as a person. Once a child develops adult thought patterns, he or she can focus on personal positive traits and accomplishments to overturn this maladaptive proverb.

The second dysfunctional family proverb impacting on my self-image as a child was "everyone will eventually abandon me." This sad anticipation of desertion is often reinforced by perceived threats. I loved my father dearly then as I do today. I feel this fear of abandonment in my case was most clearly illustrated by my anxiety that he would somehow die because of his self-destructive behavior when intoxicated. His hobbies were cars and guns. When a parent dies, a child usually accepts the tragedy as being the result of the child's behavior. The child takes responsibility for such assumptions with negative self-talk such as: "If only I had been a better kid, he wouldn't have left me." The resulting self-concept, of course, is too heavy a burden. Whether the parent dies or not, the child grows up with anxiety and guilt. Emotional maturity aids in extinguishing the self-concept, and certainly professional therapy is especially beneficial here. I struggle with abandonment issues on a regular basis.

A third family proverb which applied in my family was "you can't trust men." My father was the paramount reason for disappointment in our family dynamics. If it rained on a picnic, he was somehow at fault. This dysfunctional labeling is known as the "scapegoat" role. Daddy could have won an Oscar for his performance as the scapegoat. Taking the blame elevated his sense of guilt to an adequate level to justify a bottle of wine or a six-pack of beer. As an untreated victim of war-related post-traumatic stress disorder, his choice of medication was alcohol. Unfortunately, the negative side-effects of this commonly chosen method of escapism were perpetuated onto his children and thus led me to conclude that fathers and, therefore, men, can't be trusted. I have done my own share of dysfunctional behavior but am now determined to continue my hard work on recovery. I trust quite a few good men these days and am thankful that I have put away that nasty and untrue proverb that "you can't trust men."

The fourth and final family proverb which affected me growing up was the unspoken belief that my family and I were somehow "not normal." I misunderstood the term "normal" at that time, as I defined it to mean anyone other than myself and any family other than my own. I attached "normal" to all sorts of seemingly unattainable qualities, such as happiness and love. I envisioned it as a never-ending "Kodak moment." I watched *The Mickey Mouse Club*, "*American Bandstand*, and *I Love Lucy* and concluded that normalcy was portrayed on *Father Knows Best* and *Leave it to Beaver*. I also concluded that every house in my neighborhood was occupied by characters whose behaviors emulated our national heroes. This family proverb also proved to be untrue. We were certainly dysfunctional, but I am now convinced that dysfunction in varying degrees is the essence of every family on earth, making it more normal than abnormal. It is normal to have problems, challenges, imperfections and weaknesses. What is abnormal is to choose to stay in the self-deception of thinking life is hopeless.

Putting closure to an unhappy childhood is not easy, but the rewards of doing so are worth whatever effort is required. Two excellent practical suggestions quoted by the authors of our text, *Communicating*, are (1) "Once you start focusing on the positive, the negatives have to go away. Negative self-talk can't survive if you don't feed it"; and (2) "Positive self-talk really can turn your life around and make any life more successful" (69).

In summary, trying to recall examples of positive family proverbs when I was growing up was difficult. I simply could not remember anyone saying things like "honesty is the best policy" or "that's the way the cookie crumbles."

After concluding it would be good for my self-concept to try to remember family values, I realized that, unfortunately, my family was not strong in these areas. Recounting the four untrue family proverbs that contributed to an unhappy childhood in my case has enabled me to recognize my natural tendency to listen to negative intrapersonal communication. Continuing to work on overcoming this tendency will be my effort in the future.

Now that I've grown up, I can no longer use such flimsy excuses as "my brain made me do it." It may have worked for little Jodi, but now that I am the grandmother of Jodi's little Alex and three other beautiful little girls belonging to our son, Jason, I have dropped many of my dysfunctional family proverbs and replaced them with positive self-talk.

2
My College Stories

Tragedy Compounded

Traumatized Children, the Media, and Post-Traumatic Stress Disorder

Judy Delaney
Honors Psychology
Spring, 1999

Table of Contents

Tragedy Compounded...

Traumatized Children; The Media and Post Traumatic Stress Disorder

Tragedy Compounded

*Traumatized Children, the Media, and
Post-Traumatic Stress Disorder*

> *"The children are delicate; I will travel slowly,
> at the pace of the children."*
> – Jacob, father of many children, 18th Century, B.C.E.

The above father, a member of an ancient society, recognized the need to consider that the children were unable to maintain the same physical pace as adults on a long journey to their homeland. He therefore adjusted the pace of the entire entourage so as not to be too hard on the children. According to recorded history, this patriarch, Jacob, was father to many children whose ages were somewhere between 5 and 14 years of age. This set for us an excellent example of showing respect for children's needs and dignity. Jacob's words were recorded in the Bible at Genesis 33:13-14. It has been well established that the Bible is the most ancient, the best preserved, the most translated, and the most widely distributed book in history. Is it now imperative for us, a modern society, to fulfill our obligation to show respect for the needs and dignity of the children?

Are our children entitled to be treated as delicate? Should society adjust the pace of the journey to adulthood so as not to be too hard on the children in today's changing world? When children face trauma during the journey, are we adequately showing respect for their needs and giving them the dignity they deserve?

As in Jacob's time, so also today, parents are vested with responsibility. This responsibility, however, is always relative to the rights of the children. It is morally and legally wrong to harm children. Violent acts against children are criminal. Children can be harmed physically in ways too numerous to mention, some intentional, mostly accidental; but always with great distress not only to the child, but also to his family. Little time and attention, however, is given to the emotional well-being of the children. Violence to the psyche does not bleed. Trauma to the mind is more easily denied. We hide that which we dread, and childhood is supposed to be a happy time. Children are supposed to play, to learn, and to develop qualities that will help them become responsible adults. However, many things happen that are not supposed to happen in the journey to adulthood. A bone is broken. Proper attention is given, the body heals; the pain is forgotten. When hearts and minds are broken, does society provide the proper attention? Does the heart and mind heal? Is the pain forgotten?

TRAUMATIZED CHILDREN
"Post-Traumatic Stress Disorder (PTSD) is a condition that may develop after a child experiences a very distressing event, such as a natural disaster, violent act or sudden injury. Usually, the trauma includes a serious threat of destruction, injury, death, or other loss" (Children's Hospital Medical Center, Cincinnati). PTSD affects how the child feels and how he acts. It can appear soon after the traumatic event or weeks later. Signs may include re-experience of the trauma, such as excessive talking about the event, or dreaming about it. Withdrawal may be demonstrated by avoiding thoughts or feelings about the event, even forgetting it. There may be restlessness or agitation, sometimes demonstrated by concentration problems; and by becoming easily angered, irritable, or jumpy. Parents are advised to talk about the trauma with the child and family. The child should be reassured that it is okay to talk about the matter. In fact, talking about it can help the child to feel better. Professional sources should be utilized whenever signs of the stress in-

crease, interfere with the child's usual activity, or are present in other members of the family. PTSD is not a mental illness; it is a description of reactions to an event.

These events are of a severely traumatizing nature, like combat, rape, natural disaster, or physical abuse. These events occur also with adults and the symptoms of PTSD are the same for young and old. Children may also be angry and aggressive. PTSD can be chronic. Angry and aggressive children grow up to be angry and aggressive adults. Research shows that 40 percent of mistreated children still suffered from PTSD a year after they were first diagnosed (Children's Hospital, above). With such a high degree of continuing suffering a year after diagnosis, can we measure the suffering of the undiagnosed and untreated child?

In an article entitled "Family Violence: Children are Always the Victims" (Knowlton and Schultz), it is stated:

> *"... one third of children witnessing (domestic) violence show behavior and emotional disruptions, anxiety, sleep disruption, and school problems. Using these numbers, we can estimate that between one and three million children in the United States will suffer significant trauma affecting their ability to function effectively in society."*

Again, with such a high degree of suffering, are we considering the delicateness of the children?

Bruce D. Perry, M.D., Ph.D., states in "The Effects of Traumatic Events on Children, Materials for Caregivers":

> *"PTSD is a diagnostic label which has been traditionally associated with combat veterans. More recently, however, it has been very well described in children who have been survivors of physical abuse, sexual abuse, exposure to community or domestic violence and other children exposed to any variety of traumatic events. The three major clusters of symptoms are observed in a variety of forms of PTSD.*

In brief, however, children who survive a traumatic event and have persistence of this low-level fear state may be behaviorally impulsive, hypervigilant, motorically hyperactive, withdrawn, or depressed, have sleep difficulties … and anxiety. In general, these children may show some loss of previous functioning or a slow rate of acquiring new developmental tasks. In addition, many of these children have persisting physiological hyper-reactivity with resulting fast heart rate or borderline high blood pressure.

Whether or not someone develops post-traumatic disorder following a traumatic event is related to a variety of factors. The more life-threatening the event, the more likely someone is to develop PTSD. The more the event disrupts their normal family or social experience, the more likely someone is to develop PTSD …

Unfortunately, a great majority of children who survive traumatic experiences also have a concomitant major disruption in their way of life, their sense of community, their family structure, and will be exposed to a variety of ongoing provocative reminders of the original event (e.g., ongoing legal actions, high press visibility). The frequency with which children develop PTSD following comparable traumatic events is relatively high (45-60%).

Children who survive traumatic events and exhibit this diverse set of symptoms and physical signs are frequently also able to meet diagnostic criteria for attention deficit hyperactivity disorder, anxiety disorder NOS, major depressive disorder, conduct disorder and a variety of Axis I DSM III-R diagnosis."

THE MEDIA

I have been unable to locate specific research on what I perceive to be a secondary trauma to children suffering with PTSD, that is the psychological impact of high press visibility; especially in cases with prejudice to an individual such as a parent, sibling, or other loved one. Examples of this would include the minor children of O.J. Simpson. Losing their mother to an act of violence was traumatizing. The high press visibility with prejudice to their father would be a tragedy compounded. The privacy of children is usually protected in juvenile delinquency matters. Also, many public figures, being aware of the negative effects of high press visibility to children have recognized the need to protect the privacy of their children. There is also a concern regarding security matters such as threats of stalking, kidnapping, and so forth.

These parents, however, being of status, usually have available more sources of counsel and resources to "travel slowly, at the pace of the children." Families, however, of lesser means and inferior education on the matters of the psychiatric needs of their children fare badly in protecting their children from the sufferings of PTSD. When prejudicial high press visibility exists surrounding the traumatic events leading to the PTSD, obviously, these children's tragedies are compounded.

I propose that all children have rights to proper medical care in our country. A bleeding child is not turned away from our emergency rooms. Psychological trauma causes bleeding hearts and minds. Present efforts exist and are highly publicized regarding counseling available in school environments for school children exposed to violence. Teams are sent to the schools when high press visibility occurs to provide grief and trauma counseling. Parents are informed of resources available to aid their traumatized children and much-needed treatment is frequently utilized in these matters.

Because little, if any, research has been devoted to determining the impact of trauma to children compounded by prejudicial high press visibility and it's underlying cost factors to our governmental resources, I propose a new scientific study on this issue entitled: "Tragedy Compounded: Traumatized Children, the Media and Post-Traumatic Stress Disorder."

THE STUDY
Stating the Problem
To what extent is the traumatizing of children compounded by prejudicial high press visibility, and what is its financial cost to the American public?

Forming a Theory
It is my theory that traumatized children will have a negative impact on society if undiagnosed and untreated. I also propose that if parents and other family members are unable or unaware of proper treatment, the home environment may hinder treatment and recovery, and that upon reaching adulthood, such children will have a further negative impact on society.

The Hypothesis
I theorize that a scientific study of the cost factors will conclude that it is more cost-effective for government resources to be spent providing accessible proper treatment to children with compounded tragedy and media-related PTSD than to cover the higher costs of the negative impact on society of their behavior and emotional states.

Observation
I propose that this study be conducted as follows:
I. The Headline
II. The Family
III. The Case Study
IV. Replicating Results

I. The Headline – When a family tragedy is compounded by prejudicial high press visibility, students participating in specific college level psychology courses would contact the local school systems to arrange for traumatized children and their families to be interviewed as possible participants in the research study.

II. The Family – The family's participation in the study would be made available through the local college and school system.

III. The Case Study – The child would be observed as a case study during the remainder of his stay in the local school system. Proper treatment would be provided for only those children whose parents volunteered to participate in such treatment. Those declining treatment would be asked to voluntarily be interviewed at intervals during their stay in the school system. Those declining both treatment and participation in the study would be monitored only by behavioral and delinquency authorities, who would be requested to report only matters of public record relating to the study.

IV. Replicating Results – I would replicate results by making this a wide study in both rural and urban America and would have a minimum of two thousand participants over a period of at least 10 years.

Conclusion
Children have a right to have their physical and psychological needs met with dignity and respect. Society owes this to our children because our children are our future. Devastated minds and hearts cannot be ignored any more than a broken bone or a bleeding finger. The children are delicate. We should travel slowly, at the pace of the children.

Bibliography
Bible, Jehovah God, completed 98c.e., Genesis 22: 13, 14, Story of Jacob's Travels

Children's Hospital Medical Center (Cincinnati), Post Traumatic Stress Disorder, Patient Education Program

Knowlton, Douglas, Ph.D. and Schultz, Ryan Matthew. Children are Always the Victims, University of Minnesota

Perry, Bruce D., MD, PhD, The Effects of Traumatic Events on Children.

Materials for Caregivers, 1994, Baylor College of Medicine

Is God to Be Found Only in a Foxhole?

Judith L. Delaney
February 24, 2000
English 101H

Many who delve into the question of conversion to a belief in a personal God possessing miraculous powers of salvation will readily agree that the foxhole is an excellent place to find God. The foxhole theory of conversion comes from reports of soldiers who, having never prayed for sustenance of life to a force stronger than themselves, beg God to intercept the bullets directed by the enemy.

Of course, this theory of conversion is repeated regularly in numerous life-threatening situations.

When a person feels powerless in the face of death, he often turns to prayer. I once spoke to an atheist, who said she prayed before boarding airplanes. I asked her: "Whom do you pray to?" She responded that she didn't know, but it helped her with her fear of flying. Ironically, some prayers may even implore the highest power to use a weaker power. Such a prayer would be uttered as: "Oh, God, I'm gonna die in this foxhole if you don't send in back-up troops right now." The questions now raised are (1) did God save the frightened soldier's life, or was it the back-up troops; and (2) what about the dead soldier at his side? Did he forget to duck, or did he forget to pray? The following will attempt to establish that

God is not necessarily to be found in the foxholes we experience as we struggle along the road to life but can also be found in those beautiful, but less turbulent roadways of life that gently coax us into meditation about our human frailties and our incessant need for an almighty.

We will now compare and contrast the lives of two siblings (based on the true-life experiences of a Muslim family from Sanski Most, Bosnia). The sister lived through the ethnic cleansing efforts that spurred the Serbs to viciously attack their countrymen. The brother escaped as a refugee shortly after the outbreak of the genocide in the spring of 1992 and, therefore, only heard about the atrocities experienced back home. Their names, of course, have been changed, but their stories will aid us in appreciating what true conversion means.

Life was peaceful in Sanski Most in April 1966, when Amir Handarik and his wife, Nermina, left the Muslim hospital in Banja Luca for the pleasant 20-mile country drive home with their precious newborn daughter. The roadsides were alive with spring wildflowers as the distant mountains were blue against the sky. Everything seemed to imitate the stability of the immovable hills. Life was good in Bosnia then, and it seemed nothing would ever change.

Five-year old Aligia rushed from the family home, a wooden two-story farmhouse just outside the town. His older sisters and brother followed close behind him, anxious for a glimpse of their baby sister.

"Father, please let me be the first to hold the baba" (the Bosnian word for baby is like ours. It is pronounced "bay-ba") "I will hold her safely now that I am five. I will take good care of my baby sister, Sirma."

In April 1991, the hills of Bosnia now swayed with political unrest. Tito was dead, and Milosovic was coming to power. Nothing was the same. The future was frightening. Talk was everywhere that Bosnia must change from a province of Yugoslavia to a new country of its own. This would surely meet with resistance. Life would be dangerous. War was coming.

The Handarik family gathered at the home place to form a plan. Amir reviewed the few options remaining. "The older children have already safely immigrated to America and Italy. Aligia, you and Sirma must also flee. Take your children and go to Croatia with your older sister. She is a successful businesswoman; she'll be able to help you get established there. I cannot possibly leave with your mother now. She is sick. We will be fine here in Sanski Most."

Aligia, a prosperous merchant, was reluctant to leave his parents and his hometown, but his children were young. His in-laws from Croatia begged him to bring their daughter home, and his wife desired to be with them in Zagreb. All of this weighed heavily on his mind, but not nearly so much as his fear of fighting the Serbs. It was unthinkable that he should arm himself to kill his boyhood friends, his former classmates, over political issues. He decided to sell out. Everything he had acquired—his business, his new home, his vehicles, even his household furnishings—would be sold for one-tenth their value in the face of war to provide escape.

Sirma's husband now submitted his plan.

"It looks like war may envelop us, but I'm not sure. My uncle, the Minister of Education, does not fear the Serbs. My infant son and my five-year old daughter are safe here. Sirma and I will stay in Prijedor. I have just recently been promoted at the factory. I now supervise many workers. Our product is necessary, and I trust the local government to provide our safety. We are just a few miles from Sanski Most. Sirma and I will look after her parents. Go to Croatia, Aligia, we will come later if we must."

In 1996, in a refugee camp in Germany, Aligia and Sirma reunite after their father's death. She tells him: "Oh, my brother, I prayed constantly. Allah heard my cries for help. When the Serbs killed my husband and all the men in his family, I begged God to let me survive to raise our children. I have survived. The children are safe now and are no longer hungry as we were at Father's after Mother died. The Serbs cut off the food supply. There was no medicine for Father's asthma. No one could help us. Do you remember the Muslim family who was our neighbor? My baby cried constantly from hunger, so I went in the middle of the night to them, to beg for food; but a Serbian soldier answered the door. Our neighbor's home had also been stolen by the Serbs. I thought the soldier would surely shoot me, but he just slammed the door in disgust. I believe Allah saved me."

"My sister," Aligia answered, "I also prayed to Allah. I, too, suffered when I heard how you and our parents suffered. My thoughts of Bosnia until then were only my memories of our happy childhood and the peace with which we were so richly blessed before the war. I now have visions of what you saw, like nightmares that haunt me day and night, but they are only the works of a poor imagination. I can never see in my mind the horrors you saw with your eyes.

"When you told me how Mother prayed the Islamic prayers before she was murdered, it made me question my own faith in Allah. I asked myself: 'Why didn't He hear her?' She died because of her faith, because our names are Muslim rather than Christian. I was so distraught; I could no longer pray. I was helpless without my faith. In my fright, I got into my car and drove toward the mountains. I wasn't sure there was a God. But as I saw the blue mountains against the sky, I remembered Bosnia as it was in my childhood in the spring. I would look up toward the mountains then and think about the worries of a child. The mountains in the distance were always blue, the wildflowers would be blooming alongside the road, and I took comfort from the stability of my surroundings. The little boy in me felt close to God again as I knelt there in grief for Mother. It was so strange that I felt close to the God that I also felt probably did not exist. I was so confused. I stayed until darkness fell upon the mountains, but I found the answer, which I will now share with you, my sister.

"Mother taught us that Allah is 'watching all the people, all the time.' I no longer believe God hears the prayers of ritual, not the ritual prayers of the so-called "Christians," nor the ritual prayers of Islam. I believe that Mother was right. God is 'watching all the people, all the time.' But when He sees the children of our forefathers, Abraham from the Bible and Ismael, his son by his wife's handmaiden, to whom Muslims look as the beginning of their heritage, at war over land and policy, He turns His ears away in disgust. I don't believe He hears any prayers offered by killers because His prophet Moses taught both in the Bible and in the Quran that God gave us Ten Commandments. He commanded that His children were not to kill one another.

"I also came to realize that day, my sister, that acquiring money does not make one happy or safe. Our family, not only our blood family, but also our brothers and sisters who are all the children of God are more important than things. Life is more valuable than money, land, or the policies of men. I now believe, the same as you believe, that God listens to the prayers of those with true faith in His love and justice."

Why do People Believe in "god"?

By Judith L. Delaney

English Honors 101
Cause &
Effect Essay
March 10, 2000

What is "god"? A Bible encyclopedia *Insight on Scriptures* defines the noun "god"by stating: "anything that is worshiped can be termed a god, inasmuch as the worshiper attributes to it might greater than his own and venerates it. A person can even let his belly be his god". With this usage the capitalization is dropped. Many would question the question "What is "god"? with the response, "Why not rather ask who is God?" in that it seems more logical to think of God as a person, the Almighty, rather than as an object like a belly. The distinction between "god" the power and "God" the person would lie with the worshiper. History establishes that the majority of people over the centuries have worshiped "god" without the capitalization, that is "god" the thing rather than "God" the person. Worshipping things, things like bellies for example, may sound ignorant, especially in view of the immense knowledge now recorded, accumulated and accessible to the privileged citizens of the new millennial computer age. So why do we do it?

Is the belly a thing with might greater than our own that we should worship it? To say that anything has "might greater than our own" would be to attribute to that thing sovereignty to govern our actions. Does the belly dictate our actions? Of course it does. When we are hungry we eat. Hunger daily motivates behavior patterns such as when, what, where and how we satisfy our urges to partake of food. Hungers of the belly are certainly not the only physical governor of our actions, we also have the hungers of the need for sleep, the need for exercise, the need for shelter and every other such bodily demands that sustain our existence. We submit to these various hungers not simply to satisfy a craving, but to remain alive. One of the greatest forces ever experienced by humankind is the need for sexual fulfillment, which under all the right circumstances, is a beautiful expression of love for another person, but under the wrong circumstances, in the worst kind of situation, can become a terrifying experience, gripping a person with dread, fear and hate for a lifetime.

These "authorities" existing within our physical bodies exert great power over us, demanding that we submit or die. But, do they actually rule us as gods? No, these powers were instilled in us for our own good, to preserve us and to procreate offspring. Interestingly, these natural cravings of the body do more than simply accomplish the obvious purpose of their design. As mentioned above, who does not delight in making love at the right time, with the right person, for the right reason? Who of us would resist the thought that one of the greatest thrills a person will ever have is holding your new-born infant close to your chest as you anticipate the years of joy and happiness awaiting

you in your relationship with this tiny, yet to be discovered, person touching you so softly
and gently in your arms, but more so in your heart?

These demands of the body, however, can work to our great detriment if we so
choose. We can submit in a most unhealthy way. When we do so, we suffer the curses
of a god that drives us to destruction rather than life. When we respond with either too
much, too little, the wrong type or the wrong timing to the powers of our physical needs,
we upset the design of our bodies in a manner as counter-productive as putting sugar
rather than gasoline into the fuel tank of a car. We suffer the consequences of yielding to
the god of wild abandonment. Aren't we then worshiping a god-like devil?

If then, our physical body (a thing rather than a person) can control us either to
our benefit or our detriment, our bodies can therefore be our gods, venerated and
worshipped in the sense of submission. A first century Judean lawyer once said: "Do
you not know that if you keep presenting yourself to anyone as slaves to obey him, you
are slaves of him because you obey him . . .?" Referring to our earlier definition of "god"
as "anything that is worshipped" and to which the worshipper "attributes might greater
than his own," certainly, enslavement, or forced submission is a form of worship. If,
then the addictions or compulsions we submit to are like gods to us, what about the
compulsions of our souls, our desires which compel us to act out our emotional needs
in either beneficial or destructive manners? Our freedom of choice permits us to either
obey the beneficial strivings of our desires in a manner consistent with the positive
example of a loving creator; or, on the other hand, the negative outworkings of greed.

-4-

If we choose the latter, as history has well established to be the case for the majority

of mankind over the centuries, have we not made ourselves our "gods"? *The Jerusalem*

Bible, (1966), defining what is represented by the "tree of knowledge" from which the

first human pair partook in disobedience to their sovereign, God Almighty, states in a

footnote as follows: "[This knowledge] . . . is the power of deciding for himself what is

good and what is evil and of acting accordingly, a claim to complete moral independence

by which man refuses to recognise his status as a created being. The first sin was an

attack on God's sovereignty, a sin of pride." In choosing to become morally independent

from God, it seems our original parents chose to make themselves "gods", by submitting

to desires of greed. Parents pass on both by "nature and nurture" their errors in judgment.

Is it any wonder then that six millenniums after the first ancestors of mankind

chose to reject their "status as a created being(s)", their progeny exist in a world of

chaos and violence as nearly six billion people appear to be worshipping themselves

as "gods"?

[handwritten marginalia: God as being?]

[handwritten marginalia: Here, perhaps, you need a sentence that says that God is that (spiritual) awareness(? my words) that enables us to put our bodies & our needs in perspective, i.e. to not let our bellies/god rule us. (??)]

[handwritten marginalia: Judith: A transitional sentence, here, in which you remind us that by worshipping our bellies, we deny our bodies and forget our connection to God(?) would reinforce your thesis. Still though, this is quite clear & good! A]

Works Cited Page

"god." *Insight on the Scriptures,* Watchtower Bible and Tract Society

of New York, Inc., International Bible Students Association, Brooklyn, New

York, U.S.A., 1988

"first century Judean lawyer." *New World Translation of the Holy Scriptures,* Romans

6:16, Watchtower Bible and Tract Society of Pennsylvania, Brooklyn, New

York, U.S.A., 1984

"tree of knowledge." *The Jerusalem Bible* (1966) (qtd. in *Insight* above)

What Kind of God Is That?

Dedicated to my father, Harold H. Thompson,
a victim of World War II.

May 2000

Because we value our own lives and those of our loved ones, we can hardly reduce to nothing the value of another human life. An emotionally healthy person will do anything to preserve his life, even if it means taking another's life in self-defense. Self-defense is justifiable for killing. Nevertheless, the person doing the killing may have trouble sleeping.

A police officer in our country must feel his or her life, or that of another person's, is imminently threatened to legally pull his or her weapon. With the discharge of the weapon, an emotional toll is extracted from the officer. The intensity of the emotional trauma parallels the accuracy of the aim. If a killing occurs, the officer will get some time off as investigators carefully confirm the legality of the event, and the officer gets professional psychological treatment as necessary. Even so, the officer may have trouble sleeping. Embarking on a career requiring the use of deadly force to protect life necessitates a willingness to risk not only the body, but also the mind. According to one of my Criminal Justice professors, a retired law enforcement officer from a high-crime area of suburban Washington, DC, officers now receive instruction during training as to possible post-traumatic stress effects resulting from the use of force on the job. He stated that he personally experienced trouble sleeping for a brief period after a pedestrian wandered into the path of his cruiser and died on the scene. (Nisson)

Soldiers in war, on the other hand, are trained to kill the enemy, even when no imminent threat to life is present. Killing the enemy in a war has been considered "justified killing" by the governments of the world ever since the first war was chronicled in the first history book.

Leaders of world governments declare wars and govern the activities of the battlefield through the offices of their military. But who governs the mind, heart, and soul of the soldier who kills? Ought we not assume that soldiers who have killed may have trouble sleeping?

Lt. Col. Dave Grossman, a former Army/paratrooper and psychology professor at West Point, in his book, *On Killing*, states: "During World War II, America's armed forces lost … 504,000 men from the fighting effort because of psychiatric collapse …" It would seem, therefore, that killing could interfere with a soldier's sleep.

I am of the "baby-boomer" generation, born and raised in a small West Virginia farm and coal mining town. My father, Harold H. Thompson, of Philippi, WV, was a psychiatric casualty of the Italian Campaign of World War II. Whether he killed with a gun, a bayonet, or a grenade, I do not know. He didn't tell me. I know he was a killer because he couldn't sleep. I remember his agonizing nightmares. He screamed and struggled as though his life depended upon his overpowering a savage murderer, a German soldier, existing only in his tortured mind. Upon awakening, he realized he was back in Philippi, across the ocean from the now silent battlefield of Monte Cassino. There was really nothing to fear except falling asleep and dreaming it again. As a child, I didn't pay his screams much attention. Although they startled me from my sleep, it was a normality in our household, like living near a railroad track. After time, you don't even hear the train's whistle. I probably supposed all fathers screamed at night.

Do the government leaders and military commanders who govern the soldier's activities on the battlefield also take responsibility for his mind, heart, and soul? To some degree, they do, but the final responsibility rests with the person who agrees to become the soldier who may then become the killer. In the final analysis, we answer to ourselves for the choices we make.

My father is old and sick now and doesn't talk much about the war. If he has trouble sleeping, it's probably due more to the cancer than the war. He is my hero, not because he killed, but because he takes responsibility for the choices he's made in life. Regarding the war, he says: "I wouldn't take a million dollars for the experience, but I would go before a firing squad before going to war again." He doesn't throw the responsibility back on the government or his commanding officer. He won't even call it self-defense. He says: "I got on a boat and went across the ocean. How do you call that self-defense? Maybe in the foxhole, it was self-defense, but it wasn't self-defense when I got on that boat." He won't even validate it as a "noble cause." He says: "I think the Germans have about as much freedom today as I do here in America." Lastly, he won't say: "I did it for my God." (Thompson)

The world's governmental, military, and religious leaders throughout history have absolved guilt from the soldier's heart by the common theme: "It was the will of God." I challenge you: What kind of God is that?

World War II took some 50 million lives (of which only 300,000 were American military personnel). World War II began in 1939 when Britain and France declared war on Germany because of the Nazi invasion of Poland. Is it possible it all stemmed from a desire to further the political and commercial interests of the world powers and their rulers rather than "noble causes"? If God wanted "freedom" for the Polish, couldn't He have used a single, simple lightning bolt to take out one homicidal maniac? What kind of God would drench the mountains of Italy, the beaches of Normandy, and the waters of the Pacific with human blood spilled by human hands in the name of "freedom"? What kind of God would use an atom bomb to evaporate 80,000 lives in one flash, and do it again three days later, killing another 73,000, to halt the war? Did God cause my father's nightmares? What about the other survivors and widows and orphans? Did He wreak all that pain and suffering on the world?

The Gods of War
Myths
An ancient historian born some 1600 years before Christ recorded the first account of the psychological suffering of a killer named Cain. "... and it came to pass when they were in the field, that Cain rose up against Abel, his brother, and slew him. ... And Cain said unto the Lord, ... and if I shall be a fugitive and a vagabond on the earth, it will come to pass that everyone that findeth me will slay me." (Moses) This killer feared for his life. He anticipated retaliation for killing his brother. It wasn't long after this murder that as civilizations were established, kingdoms (governments) followed. It also was not unusual for kings to set themselves up as gods over the common people. Doing so contributed not only to their authority, but also to their power as the downtrodden could be easily deceived into believing that these men had superhuman abilities. Some even went so far as creating concepts of gods mimicking the forces of nature that demanded live sacrifices of infants to assure rain, crops, and healthy livestock necessary for sustenance of life. Of course, political conflicts arose, and kingdom fought against kingdom. The battlefields were drenched with blood as soldiers and civilians suffered. Each kingdom had its own heinous war god. Idol worship was abundant in those days. Modernists call those people pagans and their gods myths.

Abraham Lincoln's God
At his Inaugural Address delivered on March 4, 1861, President Lincoln said the following: "One section of our country believes slavery is right and ought to be extended, while the other believes it wrong and ought not to be extended. This is the only substantial dispute." After eloquently pleading for a peaceful resolution of the issue, Lincoln went on to urge his countrymen to follow the tenets of their professed faith in the God of the Bible by asking:

*"In our present differences, is either party without faith of
being in the right? If the Almighty Ruler of Nations, with his
eternal truth and justice, be on your side of the North, or on
yours of the South, that truth and that justice will surely
prevail. ... "*

He begged the people to take their time, rather than to hurry in
"hot haste to a step which you would never take deliberately, ...
[into civil war]." But the war came. And Americans spilled American blood on American soil.

On November 19, 1863, Lincoln delivered his universally recognized Gettysburg Address wherein he reminded the people that
their nation was dedicated to the "proposition that all men are
created equal" and that those buried at Gettysburg died for the
cause of a "government of the people, by the people and for the
people." In his second Inaugural Address, referring to both sides of
the bloody conflict between the now un-United States of America,
Lincoln said: "both read the same Bible and pray to the same God,
and each invokes His aid against the other ... The prayers of both
could not be answered." (Lincoln)

Lincoln is correct. The God of the Bible, the God professing to
be the Creator of human life (Genesis 2:7) *, who asserts that all
men are created equal (James 2:5-9) and incapable of self-government (Jeremiah 10:23), would no more render aid to either side
of the conflict than He would have rendered aid to Cain against
his brother. The Civil War was not God's war, it was man's. What
kind of God would snuff out 643,207 (Civil War) lives to sustain
political and commercial interests after He had already set out
the principles such as loving your neighbor as you would yourself
(Leviticus 19:18)?

*All quotations from the Bible are from the New World Translation
of the Holy Scriptures except those under "In the Name of the God
of Abraham, Isaac and Jacob," which are from the Holy Bible.

Onward "Christian" Soldiers

Prior to the Civil War, and in the decades since, nations, when called to battle enemies of the state, have been pitted against their "brothers" genetically, culturally, and spiritually. War has always been that way. Sadly, the massive killing in wars throughout history and around the globe has been condoned and promoted by Catholic, Protestant, and Orthodox churches, the main branches of Christendom. Because of this support, is it killing in the name of Christ?

The three above-named churches are the foundation stones for religion in our land. All three, as adherents to the Bible and as doctrinal believers of the Trinity, which professes Jesus to be God, are called upon to reflect: What kind of God is Jesus? Jesus himself responds in his famous Sermon on the Mount:

> *"You heard it was said: 'You must love your neighbor and hate your enemy.' However, I say to you: continue to love your enemies and to pray for those persecuting you that you may prove yourselves sons of your Father who is in the heavens since he makes his sun rise upon wicked people and good and makes it rain upon righteous people and unrighteous." (Matthew 5:43-45)*

In the Name of the God of Abraham, Isaac, and Jacob

Ancient history records the wars of the Nation of Israel and notes God's approval of the killing of the Canaanites by the heroes of modern Jews, such as Joshua and King David. Is this justification for Jews to wage war today? The God of Israel speaks for Himself at II Chronicles 28:3, where He personally accepts responsibility for the killing of those who committed the "abominable acts of the nations [Canaanites] that the Lord [He] had driven out from before the children of Israel." (The Holy Bible) Yes, Israel's God claimed to be a killer. He killed by a flood. He also drowned an army in the Red Sea. He named himself Jehovah and professes to be the Almighty God, the Creator, Owner and Judge of the universe and every living creature. If He decides to kill, would it be a course of wisdom for a man to question Him? Jehovah gave a stern warning to His people at Isaiah 1:15 when He stated: "And when you spread forth your hands, I will withdraw my eyes from you; yea, when ye make ever so many prayers, I will not hear; your hands are full of blood." (The Holy Bible) Thus, Jehovah denies involvement in unrighteous wars, those wars fought for the political or commercial interests of men.

The Wars of Allah, the God of Muhammad

The Quran directs its readers to Al'Imran [3]:3,4: "He has revealed to you the Book with the truth, confirming the scriptures which preceded it; for he already revealed the Torah and the Gospel for the guidance of men."

Holy writings must be individually searched for revelations of God's guidance for each man, as each man will stand accountable for his own actions. Direct communication with God is not the privilege of all men. It was the privilege of Musa (Moses) as recorded at Al-Nisa' [4]:164: "To Moses God spoke direct." At Exodus 20:13, God gave Moses this law: "You must not murder." Muslims must reason for themselves whether war is "holy."

Foreign Gods

The "shrinking" of our world by the advances of science and technology and our "open door" policies of immigration have brought to our land new Americans. Freedom of religion, a founding principle of democracy, extends its welcome not only to these people, but also to their gods. If called upon to wage war, each American will answer to his god, whoever or whatever he or it may be.

"There Is No God"

My friend, Sotir Vassil, of Washington, DC, related an experience he had over 55 years ago when visiting a farm in what is now the city of Rockville, MD, to discuss the Bible with a householder named Mrs. Davis. Upon introducing himself and his purpose, she fussed at him, saying: "There is no God!" He questioned how she could say such a thing, and she related that when her son was a boy, he killed a rabbit and proudly brought it to her, suggesting she cook it up for supper. Her reaction was a strong scolding as she disposed of the carcass and told him never to kill anything again. She then told Sam (my friend's nickname) that her son was now a soldier in World War II, and her conclusion was that God no longer existed. Sam's response was spontaneous as a scholar of the Bible and a lover of God: "God had nothing to do with that!" Mrs. Davis changed her mind about the existence of God. Whatever George's reasons for going to war were, I do not know, but George made the decision and must take responsibility. Sam reported to me that George was a worshipper of God. (Vassil)

Sam continues to preach about his God and, God willing, in just three more days, on May 8, 2000, Sam will become 105 years old. Sam is at peace with his God and, to my knowledge, never killed a rabbit or a person.

What Kind of God Is Your God?

None of us can escape the self-examination demanded of our conscience when we inevitably face the consequences of our choices. We must answer to ourselves, if to no one else, and take, or refuse to take, responsibility for the choices we may regret. If those choices brought pain, suffering or death to ourselves or others, in a manner incompatible with a loving God, could we dare say: "God made me do it?" What kind of God is that?

Works Cited

Grossman, Lt. Col. Dave. On Killing, USA: Little, Brown and Company, 1995

Holy Bible, The. New York: Hebrew Publishing Company (undated)

Lincoln, Abraham. First Inaugural Address. 1861

Lincoln, Abraham. Gettysburg Address. 1863

Lincoln, Abraham. Second Inaugural Address. 1865

Moses (Ancient Historian). New World Translation of the Holy

Scriptures. New York: Watchtower Bible and Tract Society of New York, Inc.

New World Translation of the Holy Scriptures. New York. Watchtower Bible and Tract Society of New York, Inc.

Nisson, Michael. Personal Interview. May 2000

Thompson, Harold H. Personal Conversations with my Father Throughout my Adulthood.

Vassil, Sotir. Personal Interview. April 2000

I AM A CRIMINAL

I am a sixty-eight year old woman and I sit in jail in Upper Marlboro, Maryland. I am convicted of harming a six-month old baby boy. I'm here by my choice. I had money in the bank for my legal defense, but I spent it unwisely. Now, I sit here for the next eight months, paying for my crime in my mind, body and soul. I deserve this. And more. I pled guilty and I should have. I deserve this. I am a criminal.

In all my life, this is the first crime for me. I'm not a criminal by nature. I grew up in Yonkers. I am normal by all standards. My family emigrated from Italy. We had our share of problems. I was born during the Depression. My husband fought in the Pacific. We raised two healthy boys. Both graduated from college and have good lives. I divorced in my forties. I'm a typical middle class American. I could be your neighbor. I could have hurt your child.

I was babysitting when I dislocated his shoulder and crushed the fragile bones near his eye socket. I babysat for thirty some years. I may have watched your child, but I only hurt the one. I don't know what happened. I was depressed. He cried. He wouldn't stop crying. I grabbed him by his arm from his infant carrier. It was on the floor by the couch. I don't know what happened. I didn't hit him. Did he hit the coffee table? I don't know. He didn't deserve to be hurt. I deserve to be here. I deserve to die.

Eavesdropping

CE2
(Due 6/24)
English 215, June 24, 2003
Creative Writing Workshop, Summer 1
Judith L. Delaney

James: Boo, are you coming to see me on Family Day? Boo, I need to see ya baby.

Cassandra: James, I got so much to do, man. The bills are due. The kids need things, I might be able to get some overtime 'cause Charles been down with the flu. If he still be down Saturday, James, I got to take his shift. You know I do.

James: Yeah, I know, baby, I know. I miss you so much. If you don't come, it's gonna be another month before I see ya, and I need to see ya. You seen or talked to my mother?

Cassandra: Went over there Tuesday after work. Ain't nothing changed over there. Your trifflin' brother been up to stuff again. He always in some kind of mess, and she just acts like she don't care. She just pays out whatever she has to and does without whatever she be needin'. Your mother got some kind of problem. Course, the new boyfriend of hers was there. He always there. Did you write that letter to your father?

James: Yeah, Boo, I wrote him a nice long letter telling him how good it was that he came all the way up here to see me. I sure hope he comes back. I never knew that man. We sat here and talked about things just like two regular men who never had any business together or anything. Just like two strangers, but Boo, I can't hate him anymore for not bein' there when I was little. Hell, I don't see my two much more than he saw me, and they live here in town. Never thought it would turn out like this, but it did. Never thought I'd be here in jail, not knowin' what the future holds and all, but it did. Boo, I'm done with the streets, I just want to be back home with you and start us a new life.

Cassandra: I want a new life, too. Big problem is, I don' know when or how you gonna be in it wiff the trouble you in now. I ax myself over and over when you gonna be out, what I gonna do till you get out. It ain't no picnic out here, JayJay.

James: Boo, now don't start. You scarin' me now. Stop that. You know there ain't nothin' I can do 'bout nothin'. We just gotta see this thing out together, baby. You my wife, Boo. You gotta stay by me now. You hear me, Boo?

Cassandra: I hear ya. I gotta go.

Note: The above was reconstructed, not from an actual telephone conversation, but from numerous letters which I had in my possession which James had written from a Virginia prison to Cassandra who was living and working in DC. The letters were written over an 18-month period beginning in the summer of 1999 and revealed nothing about the crime other than an indication that a murder conspiracy charge may be added to his other charges. James never denied nor admitted responsibility for any criminal behavior or drug or gun use. He used street names when referring to others charged with him and never implicated anyone specifically to any crime. He, in only one letter, spoke directly about the incident for which he was arrested and professed to be unaware of much of what went down. He blamed unnamed others and insisted he was just "at the wrong place, at the wrong time." I had access to Cassandra's personal property which had been placed in storage in

2001. She did not remain faithful to James; she moved on and was involved with another man. In her possessions were items indicating that she or someone else close to her was likely illegally acquiring store merchandise and using false identification.

3
My Creative Writing

Poem for Alex

Final, Original Poem 2
English 215, June 24, 2003
Creative Writing Workshop
Summer 1
Judith L. Delaney

When I look deep into your little blue eyes,
I wonder: "Who is in there?"
I see your mom.
I see your dad.
I see your Grandma Marion.
I see your Grandpa Basil.
I see myself.
But who are you, little two-year old?
You are as strong-willed as a hungry cat.
You are as observant as a detective on duty.
You have the memory of a computer.
You have the excitement of a circus.
You have the anger of the wind.
You are as bright as a photographer's flash.
And as sharp as a double-edged knife.
Why do you bite?

Armageddon

Final - Original Poem 1
English 215, June 24, 2003
Creative Writing Workshop
Summer 1, Judith L. Delaney

According to the Bible, Armageddon is God's war
Against the wicked.
God will kill everyone wicked.
God will kill everyone evil.
The wicked one will ask: "What makes me so wicked
That you would kill me?"
God will say: "You are greedy."
The evil one will ask: "Am I as evil as my neighbor?"
And God will say: "I am God. I measured the sky."
And then, the wicked and the evil ones will beg:
"Give us more time."
God will say: "I did."

Locked in Lovelessness

Final Original Poem 4
English 215, June 15, 2003
Creative Writing Workshop
Summer 1, Judith L. Delaney

How did this happen to us? Did I cause it? Or did you? Or did
   we? Or did it just decay from neglect? Or was it something
   else? Something we did not control.
Like weather?
When it's cold outside, I grab a blanket. It got cold. Why didn't I
   grab you? Why didn't you grab me?
When rain fell on us, where was our umbrella? Did we go out
   without it, like irresponsible children? Did we forget our
   raincoats, too?
We spent the whole day damp, miserable, aching, and depressed.
   An oversight?
Or was it spite?
When the storm erupted, where was our shelter? We had knitted
   no blanket of love. We had lost our umbrella of trust. We
   shared no raincoat of understanding and built no shelter of
   forgiveness.
Are we lost?
Now the sun is setting... Darkness will soon be here
Is it too late? Shall we stick together through the night? Are two
   better than one? Should I reach out to you?
Are you there?

Co-Existent Society

Final, Original Poem 3
English 215, June 25, 2003
Creative Writing Workshop
Summer 1, Judith L. Delaney

God made us to need each other.
If I refuse to embrace you, I will be cold.
I will be selfish and lonely.
But to embrace you is to trust you not to hurt me.
You, too, were made to need me. We need each other.
You must embrace me, too.
We must both crawl out on this risky limb of trust to continue to
    exist… I cannot do everything for myself, nor can you. I need
    you and you need me.
I am afraid of you; you are afraid of me. You do not know me; I do
    not know you.
Why would I hurt you when I need you? Why would you hurt me
    when you need me?
We must bridge this gap, or we will not be.
No pain, no suffering, no selfishness, no loneliness,
No life.
I must reach out to you, and you must reach out to me. I need you
    and you need me.

The Time Between the Wars

(A Fictional Short Story by Judith Delaney)

When war broke out in Europe in 1914, the world changed. Never had there been an international conflict the scale of the Great War. A small group of Christians, known as the Bible Students, had been pointing to 1914 as a year of Biblical significance. For more than 50 years, the Bible Students had preached, in fulfillment of a Gospel account prophesying that "nation would rise against nation and kingdom against kingdom," that in 1914, the world would change.

Scant attention was paid to their message by the public. Nevertheless, the "Last Days" began. America entered the Great War in 1917, crossing the ocean to battle for world dominance. More than 14 million citizens of the world were slain in "The War to End All Wars." The soldiers returned to a changed America. Normalcy, however, would not return.

The sons of many of those returning soldiers would be called upon to also cross the ocean when America would again be sucked into a tumultuous struggle for global control. Twenty short years later, war erupted once more in Europe. The time between the wars was rife with turbulence. Healing had not occurred. The fearsome Four Horsemen of the Biblical Apocalypse strode city streets, highways, and country roads throughout the land, bringing war, death, and famine to the people.

The Spanish influenza would take 200,000 lives in a single month in 1919. The Depression hit hard a decade later, bringing economic hard times on a people already awash with suffering.

America's spirit was low, but not defeated. A generation, now called the greatest by many would emerge to face hard choices: to lead, to challenge the standards, and to become pioneers at a time when change occurred at a pace causing dizziness, so rapidly that the only way to acclimate to tomorrow is to look backward to yesterday.

The State of West Virginia, nestled between north and south, neither industrial nor produce-growing, not quite Bible-belt, and not sophisticated like the urban areas just across the mountains, was like a foreign entity of its own. The culture of these folk, isolated for hundreds of years by the mountains engulfing them, produced a people proud, fierce, and determined to stand inflexible to the changes of these unsteady times. Like the strands of trees on the hills of West Virginia, the people banded together against change. Even if change were best, it would not occur without resistance.

From a small farming and coal-mining town where the rivers run together, in the north-central part of the state, came a family named Thompson. My dad, Hugh, was born third of the four hand-some, bright young men most everyone in Barbour County knew in the time between the wars. This is his story. When he died last year of cancer, he had fought another fine fight against evil. Evil has been perpetrated on good men and bad since the beginning of time. Some of it comes from the Devil himself, but most of it comes from within us, the battlefield being in our minds and hearts. The scars of war change the landscape of our souls.

My dad grew up in a small community called Mt. Liberty, out-side a town called Philippi. It's a Biblical name. The Apostle Paul wrote a letter to the Philippians. However, the Bible Philippi is pro-nounced with a long "i" at the end, but Philippi, West Virginia, ended with the sound "p" because it was named after Philip P. Bar-bour of Virginia, who served as an Associate Justice of the Supreme Court of the United States and as a member of the House of Rep-resentatives before the Civil War. Would the Philippians of West Virginia benefit from the wisdom of the Biblical apostle and the politician who served justice for all the states of the Union? If we were to ask my dad, I'm sure, being the compassionate man that he was, he would exonerate the Philippians for their shortcomings. He would say they had to learn things the hard way but came out on the other side of adversity as better persons. That's the way he would want to be judged by them.

From 1933 until the early 1950s, over 18,000 Jehovah's Witnesses were arrested, mostly in small towns and villages across America. These arrests were for such crimes as refusing to salute the flag, preaching on Sunday, and refusing to take up arms in war. Parents were arrested for not sending their children to school after the children had been expelled for refusing to salute the flag. Mob action broke out across the country, causing the Attorney General of the United States, Francis Biddle, to beg its citizens to stop the violence in a nationwide radio broadcast in 1940. He told them that "Jehovah's Witnesses had repeatedly been set upon and beaten. They had committed no crime ..." He ordered an investigation and said the mob violence would not be tolerated. He also made it clear that "Nazi evil" would not be defeated by "emulating its methods."

Even so, 1,500 mobbings occurred. In the land of the free, freedom of religion was ignored, and Jehovah's Witnesses, who professed to follow Christ, were denied civil liberties by those who would attempt to force a change of heart from worshipper to patriot. Two hundred Witnesses were jailed in South Carolina, including a six-week-old baby. A meeting place was burned in Maine. In Maryland, a mob assisted by two armed policemen broke up a meeting. In Nebraska, a man was kidnapped, beaten, and castrated. In Illinois, an entire town participated in attacking a group of Witnesses, requiring state police involvement to protect them.

West Virginia was a state that sent patriotic men to war because they also needed the work. It was also the state where, in the early twenties, coal miners fought guerilla warfare over the unionization of the coal mines. It would not escape the spirit of violence over nationalism. In Richwood in 1940, the deputy sheriff and police chief forced seven Witness men to drink castor oil, then marched them through a jeering mob to stand before the Stars and Stripes flying outside the post office. The Witnesses steadfastly refused to salute the symbol of freedom. The police in Huttonsville also participated in mob action to break up an assembly of Witnesses in Elkins. The police were arrested and paid $500 each for bail. Sometimes, when Witnesses were arrested, they were hauled off to jail on fire trucks with sirens blowing to alert the town residents that proper punishment was being meted out to these infidels of the god of patriotism.

Like the war between the states separated those who supported slavery from those who could not view another human as property, the strife of religious persecution gripping America during the time between the wars would pit brother against brother, daughter against mother, mother-in-law against daughter-in-law and father against son. Just as the Bible had predicted, a man's enemies were members of his own household.

The Thompson family was no exception. Emotions ran deep within their veins as well. Scar tissue remaining from the past intensified the pain and contributed to the pent-up anger, which was to erupt in frustration and hostility. Each brother fiercely defended his position with no less determination than a soldier refusing to give up ground fought hard to acquire. Compromise and negotiation were impossible to comprehend at that point in history, like the comprehension of one atomic bomb dropped on tens of thousands of civilians to stop the advance of soldiers in a far-away battlefield.

In the summer of 1935, Dad attended a historic convention of Jehovah's Witnesses held in Washington, DC. This convention did not relate to their stand on the flag salute, but rather to spiritual enlightenment of the understanding of God's purpose as to His placement of the faithful for eternity. Dad came home aglow with enthusiasm and zeal, the like of which would not be dampened by the ridicule of his neighbors from Mt. Liberty, nor that of the ruling class of small-town clergy, police, and politicians living in Philippi. Dad was not the only Witness in Barbour County. He and his Witness friends smelt the trouble brewing, like the old-timers claimed the "revenuers" smelt the corn-whiskey stills brewing moonshine in the West Virginia hills in those days. It just didn't faze them.

They had a message to preach; a message of salvation. Their allegiance was to God, not to a cloth representation of the nation.

My Uncle Waitman, made up of the same stuff as Dad, became the enemy of his brother. His determination to stand up in support of his government was parallel to Dad's devotion to his cause. My grandparents split as well. She felt people should mind their own business when it came to how a person decided to worship. The Witnesses were strange, for sure, from her perspective, but still harmless and deserving to be left alone. She had the same attitude about the cluster of Italian immigrants living in the company houses near the coal mines on the other side of Barbour County. Catholicism didn't suit her. Too many idols, she felt, but leave people alone, and they will leave you alone. My grandfather, on the other hand, had lost a close friend in the first war and believed his friend should not have died in vain. Patriotism was essential to protect our freedom, and freedom did not go so far as permitting dissent. Dissent would lead to loss of freedom. His line of reasoning was that wars were fought to stamp out dissent and protect freedom.

My Uncle Junior was married and had a growing family at the time. He and the youngest, Uncle William, both supported Uncle Waitman. My grandmother, although sympathetic to Hugh's right to worship as he chose, would not cross her husband. She held her tongue while her men argued and fussed at every act of disloyalty committed by the local Witnesses whose actions were promptly reported by the neighbors, likely exaggerated like clusters of grapes growing on a gossip vine.

Grandma absorbed it all and carried it word for word to her weekly meeting with Hugh down at the little creek (pronounced "crick" in West Virginia in those days), where he had a nice fishing hole under a shade tree. She would steal away on Monday afternoons with a basket of fresh-baked sugar cookies and buttermilk in a Mason jar, saying she was going to see Mirandy Wagner up on the hill. She did, too. Mirandy, old and white-haired, sat rocking in her chair on the front porch as the neighbors passed by on the dirt road, either on foot, riding a bicycle or driving a Ford Model A or a pick-up truck. They, as Mt. Liberty neighbors were accustomed to do, waved at the two women, giving Grandma eyewitnesses to her being where she was supposed to be. After leaving Mirandy, Grandma would spend some time with Hugh at the creek, finishing off the sugar cookies and giving the buttermilk to Hugh, his favorite beverage.

Uncle Junior had built a house across the road from my grandparents. Uncles Waitman and William still lived at home. Hugh had moved out shortly after the 1935 convention, hoping it would help in keeping peace at home. Sunday afternoons, he always came for dinner and stayed until dark. It was part of West Virginia culture. Families ate Sunday dinner together. Religion was not discussed at the Thompson dinner table. Religion, however, was the topic of discussion on those Monday afternoons over cookies and buttermilk under the shade tree.

Hugh knew to keep his distance from his brothers. He didn't want trouble with any Barbour Countians—and certainly not with his family. He loved and respected them, being more than willing to sacrifice being a part of the family for the sake of peace. But, just like "The War to End All Wars" was not the end of war, peace was not to be sustained for long.

In the summer of 1940, nationalistic tension was at an all-time high in West Virginia. A Witness family from the southern part of the state was engaged in a legal battle over the flag salute that would become historic. The state courts ruled against them, leading to appeals to the Supreme Court, which would also rule against them, but a mere three years later, reversed itself, establishing a precedent upheld today as one of the greatest civil rights victories ever achieved. In December 1941, the infamous Pearl Harbor attack would sink the battleship West Virginia and her sister ships, forcing America into the European war. In late summer 1940, a hayfield on the Thompson farm also became a battlefield.

The hay had been cut and dried, ready to be gathered into the barn loft on a wagon. A storm was blowing in; all hands were desperately needed to preserve the hay necessary to feed the livestock through the winter. Neighbors who didn't have hayfields were in the field. Women and children were in the field. Everyone working in the Thompson hayfield that day would never forget the fight between the two brothers.

The hay was on the wagon, and the workers were dragging themselves toward the barn when Waitman took the first shot:

"Hugh, what are you gonna do now?"

"What do you mean, Wait? I'm gonna do what we have to do now, I'm gonna get this load of hay in the barn," responded Hugh.

"That's not what I mean, and you know it! Are you gonna stick with that religion of yours now that the State Court ruled against you? Are you gonna leave it now and come home with your family where you belong? Are you gonna stop your cock-eyed ideas, which make your family the laughingstock of the county? Are you gonna stop hurtin' your mama the way you do?" challenged Waitman, his face in Hugh's.

Several of the young men grabbed the opportunity to get the wagon over to the barn and proceeded to unload it. The women gathered the children and began shooing them toward the house. The remaining men formed a circle around the two brothers. The wind picked up and dark clouds were directly overhead.

"I'm not gonna swing on ya, Wait. You'll have to hit me first if you're gonna start this. Back off, Wait! Leave me be, brother! Don't do this! Let me leave," said Hugh, trying to reason.

Grandpa and the other brothers tell the story that they tried to stop it, too. But Uncle Waitman was so full of anger and venom, there was no controlling him. He hit Dad hard the first time. Blood from Dad's nose flew sideways into Uncle Waitman's face. The second punch landed in his stomach and sounded like a baseball hitting a mitt. Dad went down on his knees. Uncle Waitman jumped forward with an uppercut knocking Dad backward onto the ground. Before the men could pull Uncle Waitman off Dad, he delivered multiple punches to his face, blackening his eyes, and cutting his lip. The men drug Uncle Waitman off, screaming and kicking like a toddler ripped from his mother's arms. He was wild.

No one—not even Grandma—could have guessed the depth of his anger at his perception of Dad's disloyalty.

They said Dad wouldn't let anyone help him up. He wanted to stand on his own power. He staggered over to his brother, now restrained by several bigger men. He came as close as he dared to his brother and said: "Calm down, brother. You calm yourself down some. Get your wits back and then, when you snap out of this fit you're havin' over my way of worship, then, brother, I'm gonna stand up here like a man. You know what I'm gonna do then, brother? I'm gonna turn the other cheek. I'm gonna let you decide what you want to do next, brother. You can kill me like Cain killed Abel if you want to, but I ain't gonna run from you, and I ain't gonna hit you back."

Everyone said what happened next must have come from God. Uncle Waitman had got his breath back, and Dad was standing up straight. Feeling likely he wasn't going to hit Dad again; the men loosened their grip on Uncle Waitman some. Just at that very second, lightning struck the tree in front of the house catching the roof on fire. Everyone sprang into action to put the fire out as the men unloading the hay got the last bit of it into the barn loft. Within a few minutes, the rain started, which put out the fire.

Dad and Uncle Waitman spent the night talking out their differences in the barn. They came to terms with each other. Dad cried like a baby at Uncle Waitman's funeral three years later. Uncle Waitman died fighting the Germans in Italy.

Liberation

English 215, June 30, 2003
Creative Writing Workshop
Summer I
Judith L. Delaney
One Act Play

Characters
Melanie Cunningham
John Cunningham

Notes

Melanie is a successful trauma room doctor in her late forties. She was born and raised in Pennsylvania in a middle-class working environment. Hard-working, intelligent, and persistent, she has always been an "over-achiever." She is connected emotionally with family, friends, and co-workers.

Her husband, John, from a well-to-do, prominent New York family, is in his sixties. He, unlike his wife, is introverted and avoids emotional intimacy by directing his attention to his successful law career in Washington, DC. They have one daughter, Susan, who is happily married and expecting her first child. John is very close to Susan, but his marriage is strained. John's son from a previous marriage, which ended in divorce, died of a drug overdose several years earlier. John is scheduled for surgery in one week. His condition is delicate.

The couple have arrived at their western Maryland vacation home in a blinding snowstorm. The exterior lights of the house are on, making the falling snow visible from the window. One table lamp is lit, and indirect lighting is on in the kitchen. The large room is a kitchen/dining/living room combination. John is sitting in the recliner. Melanie enters, carrying luggage from the car.

SCENE I
[The clock strikes 10:00.]

JOHN
Mel, why don't you just bring in what we need tonight? We'll get the rest in the morning.

MELANIE
Almost finished. Just one more trip. It's so cold in here. Even colder in the garage.
[Flipping switches on the circuit panel]
Heats on. Be warming up soon.
[Walks to stove, turns burners on]
I'm going to make some hot cocoa, want some?

JOHN
Sounds good.

MELANIE
Oh, I've got to turn the water on from the garage. I've turned on all the burners to heat things up a little faster.
[She walks back towards the stairs to go down to the garage.]
Be back in a sec …
[Glances at him]
John, you look tired, you okay?

JOHN
Yes, yes, I'm okay. I'm tired. Hope Suzie and Ed won't have any

trouble getting here tomorrow in this snow. I want to see my little girl. She's probably got a big belly by now.

[Pause]

Mel, I think I'm going to finally leave the firm behind me.

MELANIE walks to the recliner.

MELANIE

Retire?

JOHN

No, I can't get out yet, too much responsibility. No one to delegate my cases to. It's going to take me at least three years to ease out. I had been thinking I would retire in five years, but maybe I'll do it in three. I'm going to start pulling back now. I feel stressed, and this surgery has got me thinking. I guess I'm scared. For the first time in my life, I'm not sure what tomorrow will bring.

[Pause]

I know one thing; I'm looking forward to this baby.

MELANIE observes that; indeed, he looks bad, also more emotional than usual—very out of character for him.

MELANIE

It's freezing in here. You're cold. Let me warm you.

[She takes a throw from the couch and covers him, reclines the chair, pulls another one near him and draws close to him.]

John, let's talk about it.

JOHN

I'm scared, Mel. I've never really been sick. I love my work, but I also love my family. I want to see my grandchild grow up. I have some time, don't I, Mel?

MELANIE

John, Dr. Martin said your chances are good. Right now, you're tired. Martin said to come up here and relax. That's what we are going to do, just relax. Yes, slowing down is what you need to do now. It's a good idea. The baby will be here by summer. We'll spend more time together. It will be okay, John, just relax.

JOHN

When she called today, she said she had the sonogram pictures. I told her not to tell me if we have a boy or a girl until tomorrow. I want to see her face when she tells me. I would like to have a grand-daughter, just like her. Remember how she brought such joy to us? I wasn't around much when Andy was a baby. Don't even re-member why, just can't remember him being a baby.

[Now near tears]

God, he's been gone now almost three years, and I can't think about him without all this emotion. He was my son, but I can't remember knowing him. His mother made every decision for him. I guess I was working when he was small. Then, after he became an adult, it was too late. I never saw him when she wasn't there, talking for him, making decisions for him. I only saw him when he was in trou-ble. I tried, Mel, but I was never able to connect with him. I never knew him, and now, it's too late. I never will.

JOHN's emotion changes to panic as he becomes ill, has trouble breathing; she administers medical procedures.

MELANIE

John, relax, be calm …

[Lights dim]

SCENE II
[The clock strikes 1:00.
MELANIE is on the phone.]

MELANIE

I'm really okay, Ed. Don't worry about me. I'm okay. John and I both knew how sick he was. I can't say I'm surprised. We were both worried. I talked privately with his doctor, Dave Martin, a colleague of mine at the hospital. He examined John on Wednesday and again just before we left DC. Dave gave John pretty good odds after the surgery but considered the highest risk to be before the surgery.

[She pauses for ED to speak]

Dave didn't want to do the surgery until John had been on medication for a few days, and John wanted to keep our original plans with you and Susan. We all felt the relaxation prior to the surgery would be good. It was John's call to come up here. I supported him. Ed, this is going to be hard on Susan. This could not have happened at a worse time for her.

[Pause]

Yes, I've already notified the local authorities and the mortuary. The weather reports call for the snow to end soon. You and Susan decide if you'll come here and ride into DC with me or meet me there. The mortuary is sending a limo to drive me back into town and a second driver to take my car. His brother, Michael, is informing his family. I've spoken with my mother and sisters. I'll call his business associates about daybreak. Call me when she wakes, and we'll talk again then. I love you, Ed. What would I do without you to look after Susan?

[Long pause]

Bye now.

MELANIE paces back and forth a few times in front of the bay window, then stops and looks at the snow falling, illuminated by the exterior house lights. All four burners on the stove are glowing from the kitchen area in the large open room of the vacation style home. She begins to talk to herself, addressing John.

MELANIE

Oh, John, what a loss! How sad! If we had the luxury of picking our time to die—this would not have been your time. Perhaps just another six months or a year more, and you would have likely had some peace with yourself—but not now, not today. I'm sorry for you. I'm sorry for those who loved you. I'm sorry for those who depended on you, but most of all, I'm sorry for you.

You died unhappier than you even knew you were. You never gave yourself a chance at life—you knew everything except how to live. You thought it was about events and things, you never realized it was about people. You used people to achieve events and things. You made events happen, all right; you controlled so many things, but you never understood the people part. The saddest part of it all is that you never saw the people part within yourself. You smothered it so deep inside you that even you couldn't find it. You shut the people out. You shut yourself out. And now it's over; you don't have tomorrow. Tomorrow belongs to the living. It belongs to your daughter and her child; it belongs to the clients you served, your partners you exerted your every energy to please; it belongs to your mother, whom you never disappointed; your brother, whom you placed in your shadow to never excel over you; it belongs to your ex-wife, who'll gladly receive the benefits of the life insurance you carried to pay her off for the troubles you brought on her. That's not all, John, tomorrow belongs to your new law clerk, your secretary, and your janitor. It belongs to Hattie, our housekeeper. It belongs to the homeless on the street!

[Her anger rises]

And, John, tomorrow is mine! This is truly sad.

[Now in tears]

You—you of all people, you wasted your time!

[Pause, gaining control, calming down]

Who were you? I'm not sure I ever knew you myself. You seldom exposed the real you. When we met, you were different from the man who died tonight. But then again, I was not the same woman either. I suppose I probably fell in love with the vulnerable young litigation attorney suing the hospital where I worked as a resident. You swept me off my feet, all right; I was so wrapped up in my studies, I wasn't ready for love until I met you. You were so vibrant, so energetic, so needy. I loved you, everything about you. In my therapy sessions after I stopped loving you, I was able to come to terms with it. I loved you because I wanted to fill your needs. That's why I'm a doctor. At that time, I wanted to fix broken people. And you were broken. As soon as you realized why I needed you, you withdrew. You couldn't handle someone helping you. Vulnerability to you was intolerable. You couldn't handle it.

You and Carol married for all the wrong reasons. On the surface—for your family and hers, for both your careers, for the financial empires ... The media called it a "storybook wedding." That's what it was; all on the surface, no substance. Nothing beneath the cover of the storybook, no love. When you found me, I loved you, I really did. But it stopped. I'm so sorry, John, but I just couldn't sustain it alone. By the time I knew it was gone, Susan was here, and you loved her so. She loved you. I chose to stay in a dead marriage for the sake of my child.

Did I sacrifice my life for her? I guess I did. Am I sorry? No. But I'm sorry for you. You could have had us both, but you only wanted her. Was I jealous? No. I was happy that she had you. Did she know? She always knew. We talked about it at length before her marriage. She knew our marriage functioned meticulously, mechanically, by rote, oiled by money and prestige, not by love. She thanked me for my sacrifices. She thanked me for allowing the three of us to exist together in a house, rather than a home; a place for her convenience; a place where she could have us both at her fingertips when she needed either one of us; a place where, when you were preoccupied with other matters, she and I entered a world all our own, a fabulous, joyous, happy world without you. I know, John, I know. You and she also had such a world without me. You were her father. She was able to have both of us. She blossomed despite the distance between you and I, and she doesn't judge either of us that it turned out that way.

My life has not been a waste without your love. Far from it. I made my decisions. I chose my life for myself. I didn't stay for the money or your name. I didn't come into the marriage for that; I didn't stay for that. Did I stay hoping you would change? I don't know. I know I was hurt when I knew you had other women. It still hurts me. Why? I don't know. I did not expect you to be faithful. I was not faithful. Did you love someone else? Or did you use them all? I don't know.

I should have talked to you more. Every Friday evening, we had dinner out. We talked about everything except whether we loved one another. We said it to each other, especially in front of Andy and Susan, but we never talked about it to each other. We took trips, we spent time with our families, and we played the part. What was going on beneath the surface with you? I don't know.

When I first started working trauma, I had a teenager come in with a gunshot wound to the head. He died before his mother got to the hospital. I went to talk to her. For some reason, I stayed with that woman for hours. She accepted it without crying. She just wanted someone to hear about how she knew before it happened that it would happen. She said she had already been grieving long before it happened. I asked her why she hadn't been able to talk to him before it happened—to warn him, to somehow save him from himself. She said: "Oh, we talked. We talked a lot. But since I knew what he wouldn't talk about, I wouldn't bring it up. I knew what questions would make him lie to protect me, so I didn't ask those questions. That way, we only talked about the truth. I could trust him, and he could trust me. That way the talking didn't stop." After that I adopted the strategy in our relationship, and it worked. Yes, John, it worked. It worked to entrap us in a loveless marriage. I'm sorry. Maybe if I had asked more questions, things would have been different. Maybe.

[She walks toward the recliner, where John is now covered with the sofa throw, she notices the four burners on the stove still lit, she turns them off, picks up the luggage and starts to walk toward the bedroom, she turns to the recliner]

I was going to leave soon. I have been putting it off for a long time. I want someone else. I don't have anyone in mind, but I'm ready. I'm ready to move on. My career is satisfying, Susan is happy, my family doesn't need me now. I have love to give, happiness to seek, places to see and things to do, but not alone. I will not be alone.

She continues toward the bedroom.
The clock strikes two.

THE END

4
My Published Stories

God Didn't Need a Flower

God didn't need a flower, He could have had the wind and the
    rain produce the pollen,
But he knew that the beauty, the colors, and the fragrance of the
    flowers would bring joy to mankind,
So, God gave to man the flowers.

God didn't need a squirrel, He already had the lion, the elephant,
    and the camel,
But he knew the squirrel would scamper up to man and eat from
    his hand, and this would bring joy to mankind,
So, God gave to man the squirrel.

God didn't need marriage. The angels in heaven were neither
    male nor female, and they were happy. But he knew that the
    woman would complement the man and they would share a
    special love. And this would bring joy to mankind.
So, God gave to man marriage.

God didn't need babies. He could have created each man from
    the dust of the ground and brought him to life under an oak
    tree. But he knew that the miracle of birth would be precious
    and that children would cause laughter. And this would bring
    joy to mankind.
So, God gave to man babies.

God didn't need sickness, violence, pain, and death. He loved

mankind.
So. God didn't give man sickness violence, pain, and death.

God needed love. God is love. God knew that love is an expression
of free will. Man would have to choose to love. God knew that
it would not be good to create a man who could not choose
which way he would go; for then man would be just like the
animals, the vegetation, and the stars – perfect for the purpose
intended, but unable to love.
So, God created man in his image. He asked of man that he
return His love by a simple act of obedience; and man chose to
disobey.
So, man gave to man sickness, violence, pain, and death.

Gid didn't need the Bible. He had all the knowledge and wisdom.
But he knew man would stumble along the way and need a
light for his roadway; and this would guide mankind.
So, God gave man the Bible.

God didn't need a ransom. He had not sinned. But he knew man
was lost to imperfection and sin and could not buy back his
life. God wanted man to live.
So, God gave man his Son.
God didn't need hope. He knows the outcome of all things. But he
knew man would suffer; would be unable to agree; there would
be wars; famine would come; man would be hungry; man
would be greedy and would take advantage of his fellow man.
Man would love pleasures and alcohol. Drugs would dull his
brain. A child would be born deaf and not hear the music; or
blind and not see the colors. A baby would be born and die
before it's mother could cradle it in her arms or hear its cry. A
man would get cancer and feel unbearable pain; or get old and
tired. God knew a righteous woman's son would be wicked and
her heart would break.

He knew that man would need hope; and so, He said: "The earth shall stand forever and the meek shall inherit the earth. My will shall be done on earth as it is in heaven. The dead will arise.

Knowledge of me will fill the earth. The lamb will reside with the lion and a little boy will lead them. Wars will cease. I will wipe every tear from their eyes and death will be no more; neither will mourning, nor outcry, nor pain be anymore". This would bring joy to mankind.

So, God gave to man hope.

God didn't need comfort. He knew His purpose was soon to be fulfilled. But He knew time would pass slowly for mankind. Man would need a reminder of His love and His promise.

He knew that the flowers would bring joy to mankind.

So, God gave man the flowers.

Published in "The Bowie Times",
August 1985, edited September 2019

Something Worse Than A Sniper's Bullet

Judy Delaney, Opinion published in the Owl

Today, November 1, 2002, isn't just another ordinary day. Although the sun is hiding behind the clouds, it's a day to celebrate life, a day to hold our loved ones closer, and a day to call your mate or your child "sweetheart" with even deeper affection. It's a good day to call Grandma just to tell her you're thinking about her; a good day to thank a dedicated professor for the extra effort to clarify a complex lecture. Maybe it's even a good day to smile a little more often, especially at strangers in the hallway. The best thing about today is that we can turn the calendar page and try to blot out what for many Washingtonians has become "Black October".

The cold recognition that every single one of us was the possible target of a psychopathic stalker bent on killing people as if they were rats on the street was chillier than the nippy weather today. Leaving behind little more evidence than the carnage, a tarot card and the very important "marked" bullets connecting him to the kill, he made it hard for the 1000-member law enforcement team to finally catch him. But catch him they did. His game is over. His adventurous spree into the annals of crime is over.

Oh, sure, his name and face will be on the media today and in our criminal justice textbooks next year, but I won't put his name in this article. I'm sick of him. I won't even dignify his youthful companion in evil with a separate identity. It seems to me that kid was just another part of his arsenal. In reflection, I wonder if maybe the older guy was just a part of someone else's arsenal, someone even bigger and badder than him to whom his name is nothing significant.

But today's a new day. Although the paper still screams violence from the headlines, we also have good news to embrace. Although many people will die today of violence, sickness and aging, many people will also be born today to become peacemakers, healers, and lifelong contributors of good. The Biblical writer Solomon, considered to be the wisest man of his day, gave us good advice when he said, "Better is it to go to the house of mourning than to go to the banquet house, because that is the end of all mankind; and the one alive should take it to his heart." The suggestion is that when we enter "the house of mourning", such as we've been forced to do during this past month of sniper killings, we take to heart that mourners will someday be mourned, that life ends in death and that the living have a limited opportunity to be as happy as they choose to be. Having a future and being in control of it is what separates us from the sniper.

The thing worse than a sniper's bullet is being the sniper. It's all over for him. Anything he ever had is now gone. Will his children still love him? The rest of his natural life, however long or short it may be, is tarnished with guilt if he has a conscience. If he doesn't, that is, if he is a true psychopath without a conscience, he also lacks ability to love. What kind of life is that? —-he may as well be an animal, like a rat on the street. If he is the pawn of someone bigger and badder than himself, he may as well be an inanimate object, like a .223-caliber semiautomatic rifle. If that's the case, he's broken and useless now that he's in custody, so he'll be discarded like trash. If he happens to be a human like us, rather than god as he claims, he'd better pray to God for the mercy he denied his victims.

Yes, indeed, being a sniper is worse than being a victim. Being alive is the best thing of all.

Too Many Dead Babies

Last semester my Speech 101 professor instructed us not to use "too many dead babies" in an introduction to a persuasive speech. She said that most people are really turned off by the mental image of dead babies and if you say it too often, it can be interpreted as over-kill. Oops! Better drop "over-kill."

Well, wish I could erase some of the horrific images I have now painted in your young minds. But, "too many dead babies" is the issue. Five dead babies whose faces you may have seen recently on the news were Noah, John, Paul, Luke and Mary Yates. Perhaps it's time we focus on the innocent victims. Their mentally ill mother, who according to the jury, although seriously impaired, knew what she was doing, drowned these children in the family bathtub. Her name doesn't matter now. She'll spend the rest of her life locked up. The father's name doesn't matter much either. He can't save Noah, John, Paul, Luke or Mary now. According to him, it wasn't his fault. An Associated Press article dated March 15th quotes him as asking: "How could she have been so ill and the medical community not diagnose her, not treat her, not protect our family from her?" Seems like he sees himself as the victim. But, at least he's alive, alive enough to even consider suing the doctors, getting a divorce, marrying again and having more children. Life goes on.

If you're still up to it, I'd like to talk about some more dead babies. Another dead baby was Daniel Reardon, a Maryland freshman, who died last month after being found unconscious in front of a fraternity

Student Viewpoint
Judy Delaney

house. Six months before that it was Alexander Klochkoff, a Maryland sophomore, who was found dead in front of a fraternity house. Just like the mother who drowned her kids, these students were "seriously impaired". Alcohol was involved in their impairment. The mother's impairment may have had something to do with her not taking drugs to prevent psychosis. Now that we are on the subject of drugs and dead babies, I'm sure each of you can paint your own mental image of someone you knew who became a dead baby by becoming "seriously impaired" on drugs. Irresponsible behavior can kill you and innocent victims who wander into your path when you are "seriously impaired".

Wouldn't it be nice if we could all just grow up and take responsibility for ourselves and those who depend on us?

Judy Delaney writes play reviews for The Owl.

Approximately thirty years after the death of Jesus, his apostle known as Paul gave admonition to the Christian congregation in Colossae to readjust their behavior. Specifically, he told them to stop such practices as "anger, malice, wrath and blasphemy." He continues in his letter (chapter 3, verse 9) to state; "Lie not to one another, seeing that ye have put off the old man with his deeds." (King James Version) The translators of the King James Bible concluded their work in the year 1611 and literally translated the word "man" for the Greek word "anthropos" used by Paul. A modern translation says, "strip off the old personality" as though we can change it like we change our clothes. Definitions of the word "personality", which include such terms as "a person's distinct character" (Oxford) and "that which constitutes an individual" (New Webster), clearly permit us to conclude that Paul expected the people of Colossae to make some major changes in what psychologists today might define as personality. The interesting question arises now as to whether a person can become a "new

PERSONALITY - NATURE OR NURTURE?
Judith L. Delaney

man" (or "woman")?

This would be a near impossibility for the proponents of the nature theory who perceive personality to be a product of genetics. Changing one's genetically determined personality would be as hard as changing one's skin or eye color. Of course, modern science, in pursuit of the same Fountain of Youth, which inspired ancient discoverers of new lands to risk lives and fortunes, has provided us with sun-tanning lights to change our skin color and contact lenses to change our eye color. Unfortunately for the Colossians, science only recently started to work on personality. And, the studies so far are indeed impressive and convincing that we may get our nasty temper from Uncle Joe and our patience from Grandpa Job. The famous Minnesota Twin Study as well as the 1990 Waller research indicate that, although a specific personality gene remains undiscovered, we cannot discount that persons sharing very similar genetic make-up have similar personalities.

The studies supporting nurture, on the other hand, also are convincing that personality is shaped by exposures to our environment. Children do tend to adopt their parents' customs, lifestyles, politics, religions, recipes, housekeeping habits, and attitudes. My mind's eye requires no stretch to envision little angry, malicious, wrathful, blasphemous Colossian children imitating their parents. If the Colossians didn't get a grip, it would easily explain why the family two doors down can't get a grip - their ancestors arrived at Ellis Island on the boat from Colossae.

In summary, I see no point at all in continuing to risk life and fortune in pursuit of resolving the debate between nature and nurture. We get our personality from both our genes and our environment. I suggest we spend our time and funds studying ways to acquire a "new personality" by giving up harmful, maladaptive behavior patterns, breaking bad habits and practicing healthy, positive activities that contribute happiness to others and ourselves.

Judy Delaney is an Owl staff writer.

Precauciones simples bajo el sol

Por Judith Delaney

El verano ha llegado. El sol mexicano está que arde. ¿Deberías preocuparte por sobreexponerte al sol?

Sí. Según la Organización Mundial de la Salud, el aumento de casos de cáncer de piel está fuertemente relacionado con la sobreexposición a la luz del sol.

También está reportada como la causa fundamental de daños en la piel, ojos y el sistema inmune. Protegerte de radiación ultravioleta dañina es muy sencillo.

Primero revisa el índice de UV (ultravioleta) en http://meteo-vista.com. Por el momento, está en su máximo nivel (11+) en Tequisquiapan.

Aplica estas simples precauciones para protegerte de la sobre exposición.

Limita el tiempo en el sol de mediodía, permanece bajo un techo entre 10 y 4.

Busca la sombra, camina debajo de árboles y a la sombra de edificios, usa sombrillas.

Usa ropa protectora, viste sombreros, lentes de sol y ropa suelta.

Usa bloqueador solar, aplica SPF 15+ y re-aplica.

Sé prudente protegiendo a bebés y niños pequeños porque tienen piel más delicada.
Disfruta el sol, pero ten cuidado.

Simple precautions in the sun

Summer has arrived. The Mexican sun is hot. Should you worry about sun overexposure?

Yes, according to the World

Health Organization the rise in the incidence of skin cancers is strongly related to overexposure to sunlight.

It is also reported to be the underlying cause of harm to the skin, eye and immune system. Protecting yourself from harmful ultraviolet radiation is simple.

First check the UV (ultraviolet) Index on-line at http://www.meteo-vista.com. At the moment, it is at the highest level (11+) in Tequisquiapan.

Use these simple precautions to protect yourself from over-exposure. Limit time in the midday sun - stay indoors between 10 and 4.

Seek shade - walk under trees and in the shade of buildings, use an umbrella.

Wear protective clothing - wear hats, sunglasses and tightly woven, loose-fitting clothes.

Use sunscreen - apply SPF 15+ liberally and re-apply.

Be very careful to protect babies and young children whose skin is more delicate.
Enjoy the sun, but be careful.

PUBLISHED IN TequisMagico April 17, 2014

Why is Mexico Getting So Fat?

A recent United Nations report indicates that Mexico has now surpassed the United States in it's rate of adult obesity levels. Some blame Mexico's neighbor to the north for this new worrisome statistic. 32.8% of Mexicans are now considered obese. It has been said that Portifiro Diaz said: "¡Pobre México! ¡Tan lejos de Dios y tan cerca de los Estados Unidos!" (*Poor Mexico, so far from God and so close to the United States*).

John D. Sutter, CNN, contacted Dr. Juan Rivera, a director at Mexico's National Public Health Institute to ask him if the US is making Mexico obese. Sutter reported: "Dr. Rivera didn't blame the United States, but he did blame "sugary beverages," which the United States produces and markets." According to Rivera, the average Mexican drinks 163 liters of sugary beverages per year", the highest consumption in the world. The American culture of fast food and super-sized portions obviously has a strong influence, not only on Mexico, but on countries around the globe. Also American food and drink business giants sell vast quantities of unhealthly pre-packaged food conveniently to Mexican importers.

What else could be making Mexico so far? Could it be that Mexicans are getting less exercise, that poorer Mexicans are eating cheaper junk foods, while the rising middle-class in Mexico is eating more foods saturated in carbohydrates? The possibilities are endless — but, in truth, the reality is simple. Mexico is not alone in facing this serious health challenge. According to the same report, 1.4 billion people worldwide are overweight and 500 million are obese.

It doesn't matter if your workmate, your neighbor or people in any country in the world are obese, what matters is how you, whether you are at a normal weight, overweight or obese, take personal responsibility for your health and how you make the best possible eating choices.

PUBLISHED IN TequisMagico August 27, 2013

5
Family Mementos

november 22 1966.

This locket is for
    Judy Delaney. its fifty years
old now;   and as bright as the day I got it
She bought a real expensive
chain for it.
                              Signed
    Grand ma Iris

The Thompson Boys Pick and Sing

Hugh, Junior, Gearl, William and Bob

Valley Dale

Judith Thompson Delaney - Front Row, 6th from left
Gary Thompson - Second Row, Last Boy from Left
Teacher - Uncle Bob Thompson
Lunchroom Cook - Dora Fisher

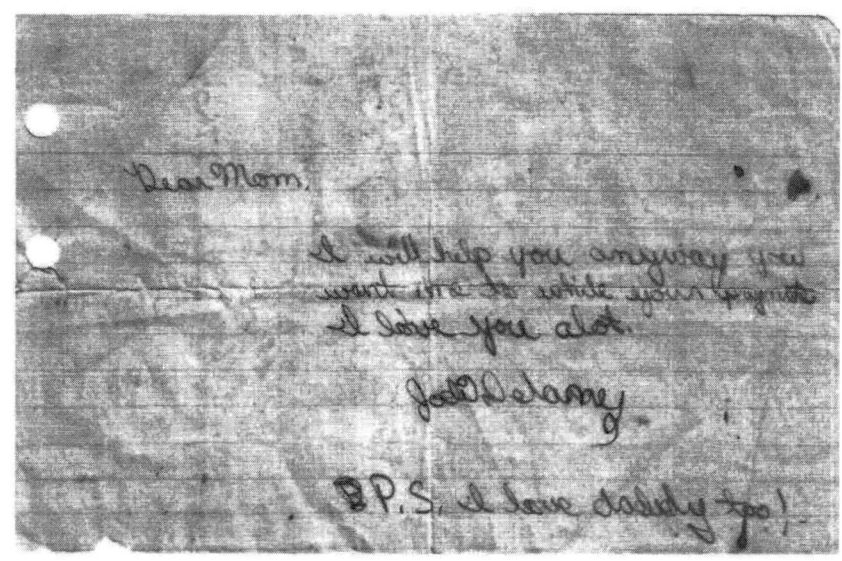

Dear Mom,
I will help you anyway you want me to while your pregnet.
I love you alot. Jodi Delaney
P.S. I love daddy too!

hola Gramma y grampa! I hope everything is going well in Mexico! I miss & love you both. I've been practicing español so we will still be able to communicate when you come home.

    Te amo,
     Brianna

¡me gustas! ♥ Kaitlin

salsa

¡hola!

Chalupa

{taco}

Nachos

¡YUM!

If I were in Charge of the World
By: Alex Caramanico

If I were in charge of the world, I would click the delete button and it will permanetly delete girls. I would terminate allergies and wars.

If I were in charge of the world, I would bring every meat-eating dinosaurs only. I would make a lot more vidio games and PIE.

If I were in charge of the world, I'll give kids freedom to go where ever they want any time and make a MILLION times MORE PIE then usual. I would eliminate vegetables and rules.

If I was in charge of the world Monday through Thursday mornings would be no more. I would burn all spices for tea, make TELEPORTATION abilities to go to any place in the Universe.

and a person who forgot to pay and forgot to play. Would still be in charge of the world.

6
The Legal Stories

The Crying Killer

CJT 254
Evidence and Procedure Spring 2000
Honors Contract Credit Portfolio
Judith L. Delaney, May 14, 2000

My name is Judith Delaney. I am an ordained minister, a wife, mother, and grandmother. I have a cat named Cyrus. I am a college student pursuing a degree in paralegal criminal justice with a focus on psychology. In the future, I hope to use my degree in the fields of law enforcement or defense law.

I am also the daughter of a killer. My father was a psychiatric casualty of his participation in World War II. The resulting post-traumatic stress disorder made him cry.

During this semester, I was contracted to do honors credit work in Criminal Justice Course 254, Evidence and Procedure. A part of my contract was to follow the Circuit Court criminal trial entitled Maryland v. Worthy. In April 2000, Mr. Worthy took responsibility for a killing by pleading guilty to second degree murder in exchange for a 25-year sentence. In the courtroom, I watched Mr. Worthy cry. It would be the second time he cried; the first being when he gave his confession.

After being arrested on another charge in the summer of 1999, Mr. Worthy spoke to another inmate about his involvement in the murder case. That inmate, to get a plea bargain, reported Mr. Worthy's discussion to the police. During his interrogation, Mr. Worthy signed a lengthy and detailed confession. He would later claim that, due to his being physically assaulted in the interrogation room and not being able to read and write, he permitted one of the two detectives present to write the confession, which he said he signed under duress. The hearing I attended was his effort to have that confession thrown out. I will read from the transcript of his testimony which occurred on January 11, 2000. On the stand, the state's attorney is questioning Mr. Worthy about his confession:

STATES ATTORNEY: Okay. And when Detective Robertson—you saw him testify, right? You recognize him?

WORTHY: Yes.

STATE'S ATTORNEY: When he came to talk with you, what happened?

WORTHY: He told me what, basically what happened, and then he was like trying to get me to write a statement. And then he was like—I was like, I want my attorney present. I say, if I can't have my attorney present, let me call my mother. And they wouldn't let me call her. And I said, well, give me a public defender. I don't want to talk about it. You know what I'm saying? And they wouldn't do it.

STATE'S ATTORNEY: Did there ever come a time when Detective Robertson threatened you in any way?

WORTHY: Yeah. When Detective Walker brung him in there, Detective Walker walked back out. Detective Robertson had a briefcase thing, set it on the table and he had some cord or something with it. And he was saying something about this was a lie detector machine or something. It was a voice—it goes by your voice or something. And then he was like, he wanted me to talk through that. I was like, I ain't saying nothing. And so he was saying a couple things and then I was like, man, I ain't got nothing to say to you all until I have my lawyer present.

And he was like, you one of those Billy Bad Guys out on
the street, I guess. I was like, I ain't no dummy. Because
he was standing up in my face, his knee was between my
legs hitting on the seat, and I was getting mad. And, you
know, I had tears coming out of my eyes, and I was
handcuffed to the wall still. And I was just like man,
look, I ain't writing no statement. And you know, he kept
going on and on. And finally, I just said that I did it.

STATE'S ATTORNEY: Why did you do that?

WORTHY: So I can hurry up and get out of there, so I can
come here, so they can go ahead and bring me to the de-
tention center, so I can call my attorney.

My Evidence and Procedure class discussed this testimony, and
the professor indicated it was the defendant's effort to explain the
reason for his crying during his interrogation by the homicide
detective.

The remainder of the testimony that morning related to the defendant's claim that he was unable to read or write and so could not
have verified that the confession was accurate before he signed it.

There was a lunch break, and when the defendant returned to
the stand, the confession was given to him for discussion and
further questioning. Contrary to his claim of being unable to read,
he read parts of the confession when questioned.

STATE'S ATTORNEY: All right. From there you say, from
there the statement says on page four, 'He told me if
anyone would come inside, I knew what to do.' Is that
right? Please look at the statement. Do you see where I
am?

WORTHY: Yeah

STATE'S ATTORNEY: All right. Is that your answer to
the—part of your answer to the detective?

WORTHY: Somewhat.

STATE'S ATTORNEY: Somewhat?

WORTHY: Derrell, it was, basically, he wanted me to let him know if somebody was coming in the building. It wasn't—

STATE'S ATTORNEY: 'So I was standing there with the gun behind my back.' Do you see that? Please continue to read the statement with me, Mr. Worthy, please. Do you see that line there?

WORTHY: Yes

STATE'S ATTORNEY: Is that part of your answer, sir?

WORTHY: (no response)

STATE'S ATTORNEY: Please continue.

WORTHY: And that's not me right there.

STATE'S ATTORNEY: That's not your answer?

WORTHY: No

STATE'S ATTORNEY: All right. So, the detective came up with this: 'I had the gun behind my back.' Is that right?

WORTHY: Like I said he wanted me to testify against Derrell, write a statement against him. I told him that I did it to get this stuff over with, so I could go call my lawyer. He pretty much write it how he wanted to write it.

STATE'S ATTORNEY: Uh huh. Well, Mr. Worthy, what I'm trying to do is figure out what is true in the statement and what's untrue. So that's what we're doing. So, I'm going down at the point where it says, 'About three or four minutes later'—do you see that about halfway down the page, sir?

WORTHY: Yeah.

STATE'S ATTORNEY: 'About three or four minutes later the girl came in.' All right. Is that part of your answer? Did you tell the detective that?

WORTHY: Yes.

STATE'S ATTORNEY: 'She saw the apartment door open and started screaming, yelling and running toward me,' Is that part of your answer?

WORTHY: Yeah.

STATE'S ATTORNEY: Yes. 'I pointed the gun and started
    firing.' Is that part of your answer?
WORTHY: Yeah.
Victim's mother screamed: "You killed my child!"
(Disruption in the courtroom.)
(Pause in proceedings.)

When the victim's mother screamed: "You killed my child!" The
judge called the attorneys to the bench for a conference. A recess
was not called. Mr. Worthy was left to wait several minutes on the
witness stand, and he cried.

Are tears a proof of guilt? No. Do killers cry? Yes, there is always
a psychological price to pay for taking a human life. This is true
whether the killing was self-defense, in wartime, an accident or a
murder.

17-YEAR-OLD IS SHOT TO DEATH, *STEPFATHER* INJURED IN *OXON HILL*

Sunday, December 31, 1995 ; Page B03

A 17-year-old girl was shot to death and her *stepfather* was critically wounded
yesterday afternoon in an attack in *Oxon Hill*, Prince George's County police said.

The two were shot multiple times about 4:30 p.m. in the 1500 block of Iverson Street,
police said. The 42-year-old man was taken to Prince George's County Medical Center,
where he was in critical condition last night. His stepdaughter was pronounced dead at
Greater Southeast Hospital.

Police did not release the names of the two because the *stepfather* is a witness.

Police said they know of no motive and have no suspects in the attack.

*Articles appear as they were originally printed in The Washington Post and may not
include subsequent corrections.*

Religious Freedom and the State of Maryland

Maryland State Constitution, Article 36:

"That as it is the duty of every man to worship God in such manner as he thinks most acceptable … wherefore, no person ought by any law to be molested in his person or estate, on account of his religious persuasion."

Judith L. Delaney, CIT 151H
Intro to Criminal Justice 100
Fall 2002

Introduction

Approximately 500 years before the birth of Christ, an elderly, high-ranking government official deliberately and openly committed a capital offense. He was immediately sentenced to death.

The defendant, who had immigrated to the country as a lad, was a trusted confidant of the king, but unfortunately, he was also the hated rival of his governmental peers. It was those jealous high officials who had cleverly teamed up to fashion a new law with the specific intent of disposing of him. The new law had been quickly enacted and published to the people. Special legal language was written into the law to make annulment constitutionally impossible. Even so, the king himself took up the legal defense of his beloved friend. The account of King Darius' fruitless efforts reads as follows:

> *Consequently, the king, as soon as he heard the word, it was very displeasing to him, and toward [the defendant] he set his mind in order to rescue him; and till the sitting of the sun, he kept on striving to deliver him. (New World*

Translation of the Holy Scriptures, Daniel 6:14)

The story of "Daniel in the Lion's Pit" is familiar to many Americans. Daniel's crime was praying. The law read as follows: "Whoever makes a petition to any god or man for thirty days except to … [the] king should be thrown to the lion's pit" (Daniel 6:7). The Babylonian law in this instance was hardly the first law criminalizing worship.

The nation of Israel by adopting the Ten Commandments approximately 1,000 years prior to Daniel's exile to Babylon established the death penalty for idolatry. God set up a code of worship at the same time He established humanity. Unfortunately, the problem of establishing equitable laws regarding religion continues to plague us today as it did in ancient history.

Way back then, very few religious persuasions existed. Today, one can choose from an ever-growing smorgasbord of religious philosophies and creeds permitting the worship of any god, any person, or anything. For that matter, even "creedless" religions are available, allowing one to establish a form of worship unique to the individual's desires. And, what about those who choose to be non-religious? In a democracy permitting freedom of religion, shouldn't the agnostic and atheist be free of religion?

All this confusion and complexity presents a legal minefield for legislatures of democracies. The challenge is to encompass equitable laws respecting religious liberty for all faiths (and the faithless) with adequate laws necessary for the maintenance of freedom, peace, and order in a multicultural, diverse society.

We will now visit the legislative history of religious freedom and tolerance in Maryland. We will start with the founding of the colony by the Catholic proprietor, Lord Baltimore, and move to the more modern State and Federal court decisions that form the touchstones of religious freedom. We will proceed to very current media reports relating to the complex flux of legal issues existing between the very religious, the secularly religious, the barely religious and the non-religious citizens of Maryland and her sister states. We will then arrive full circle back to Daniel's day where we will be forced to recognize that, although the Founding Fathers of the "Free State" correctly recognized that "… all persons are equally entitled to protection in their religious liberty…" (Article 36, Maryland State Constitution), it is impossible for humans to legislate and enforce true religious liberty. It is therefore necessary, as it was with Daniel, that each person decide individually whether to submit to a law imposed upon his religious conscience or accept the subsequent consequences.

The Colony for Religious Freedom

In 1617, George Calvert was knighted in the Court of King James, a Protestant, of England. In 1624, Calvert became a Roman Catholic. He was given the title of Lord Baltimore when he resigned his position of high political influence to establish a new colony in America where Catholics could escape the harsh persecutions they were experiencing in England. He visited the New World in 1628, selected the location of the colony, and returned to England to petition the new monarchy King Charles I for the grant of land. George Calvert died on April 15, 1632, leaving his title to his son, Cecelius, who received the charter to the colony from King Charles I the following June.

The new colony was named Maryland in honor of Charles' wife, Queen Henrietta Maria, daughter of Henry IV of France. Cecelius Calvert remained in England to administer the affairs of the colony there. He named his brother, Leonard, as governor. (Maryland Catholics on the Frontier – A Summary (2))

One hundred and forty souls departed England for Maryland on November 22, 1633. Although two Jesuit priests were among these brave travelers, only 40 of the colonists were Catholics. (Credo (1))

Lord Baltimore, in the opening paragraph of his instructions to the governor and commissioners, warned the early settlers that they were not to give offense to one another in matters of religion, either during the voyage or in the new colony. (Maryland State Archives (4))

One of the Jesuit priests consecrated the colony to St. Mary of the Immaculate Conception and the first capital was named St. Mary's City where the colonists erected a "great cross" (Maryland State Archives (4)). Initially, Catholics and Protestants shared a single chapel.

The Maryland State Archives reports two incidents of religious intolerance:

> *... The first religious dispute, so far as we know, had occurred in 1638, when one William Lewis, a Catholic, had been charged by his Protestant servants with proselytizing by force of his authority, thus provoking a quarrel over religion. Lewis, tried by a court predominantly Catholic had been found guilty and fined 500 pounds of tobacco. Similarly, in 1641 a Thomas Gerard, also Catholic, had been charged with taking the keys of the chapel from Protestants and removing their books from the building. Again, a Catholic had been declared guilty of interfering in the religion of Protestants and, with a nice irony, the court had decreed that Gerard's fine of 500 pounds of tobacco be held for the support of the first Protestant minister who should arrive in the colony. (1)*

In 1649 the Maryland Provincial Assembly adopted the "Act Concerning Religion," which stated in part: "No person in Maryland professing to believe in Jesus Christ shall henceforth be in any way troubled, molested or discontinued for or in respect of his or her religion ..." (Maryland State Archives (2))

Unfortunately, religious tolerance was to be disrupted only five years later when zealous Maryland Puritans repealed the Act after being inspired by the rise of Puritan power in England. "The Act of Toleration" came back in force after the Puritan regime fell in 1661.

A second act of religious toleration was legislated in 1825 permitting non-Christians to be officeholders in Maryland. Although the bill established extended political rights to Jews, it still contained language requiring that an officeholder profess belief in a "future state of rewards and punishments." (Maryland State Archives (8))

Serious trouble erupted for faithful Catholics in 1692 when William of Orange, the victor of the Protestant Revolution in England, made the Church of England the state religion not only across the Atlantic, but also here in the colonies. Maryland Catholics, who had always been in the minority, now became objects of persecution as they lost political offices, churches, and schools, the right to vote, and the right to sit on juries. They were taxed to support the Church of England. Many Catholics moved west to such locations as Pennsylvania, Ohio, and Kentucky.

The Birth of a New Nation Respecting Equality and Freedom

Marylanders today have strong reason for pride in that our legislative history clearly establishes Maryland as the earliest and most significant contributor to the cause of religious freedom on American soil.

This distinction essentially belongs to the first Lord Baltimore, Sir George Calvert. Maryland State Archives comments as follows regarding this noble and courageous pioneer of the First Amendment to our present federal Constitution:

> *Twenty years of service under the secretary of state [and] directly under the king, had made Calvert into one of the ablest diplomats of his time. In 1625, however, at the height of his career, it became clear that Parliament was determined to disqualify Catholics from any position of trust or profit. At this moment, Calvert ... chose to announce his conversion to the Catholic faith - an act that forever acquits him of any charge of insincerity.*

Historians, while frequently praising George Calvert's faithfulness to his religion, have seldom pointed out the significance which his change of faith may have had on his philosophy of government. There was already in Calvert's mind a sharp and complete distinction between religion and politics. He had separated church and state in his thinking long before he and his son attempted to separate them in his colony (Cecilius). Calvert made certain also that his enemies would have no cause to attack his charter on the basis of religion. By implication the document stated that the same pains and penalties prevailing in England would be imposed upon the Lord Proprietary if ever he should allow prejudice to "God's Holy and True Christian Religion"—a statement sufficiently broad to satisfy wide interpretation. As a practical man, he mentioned no particular faith in the charter, by virtue then of the vagueness of the charter and its failure to mention particular faiths, a policy of religious freedom was to be expected in Maryland.

The purpose of the vague religious clause in the charter he perceived with the utmost clarity was to prevent a repetition in the colony of the unhappy religious and political troubles prevalent in England. Accordingly, he made every effort to impress upon his settlers the necessity for avoiding religious controversy. (3 & 4)

A century and a half would pass after the first Lord Baltimore planted the seeds of religious tolerance in the rich soil of the New World, 3,000 miles across the ocean from the Mother Land before the colonies would declare independence and form a federal government over state and local governments. Religious intolerance and discrimination might have remained in the hearts of those so disposed (with occasional eruptions into criminal violence), but blood would not spill in civil war in America over the choice of worship as it had previously in Europe. The new federal constitution would establish the equality of all men and guarantee freedom of religion.

Court Decisions
The Constitution of the United States vests legislative powers in Con-

gress and judicial powers in the Supreme Court and courts of appeals, both federal and state. According to Article III, Section 2, this judicial power was to extend to "all cases in law and equity." These provisions essentially allow law to either be enacted by legislature or established by common law or case law. Over the past two centuries, the courts have ruled on numerous legal issues relating to freedom of religion. Some of the more salient points are discussed here.

Watson v. Jones (1872)
Church disputes were held to be beyond the bounds of civil courts.

Minersville v. Gobitis (1940) ; West Virginia v. Barnette (1943)
The Supreme Court ruled in *Minersville* that a public school could require Jehovah's Witness students to salute the flag and pledge allegiance to it even if doing so violated their religious liberty. The children were expelled from public schools. The *West Virginia* case, brought also by Jehovah's Witnesses overturned the *Minersville* case and permitted students to refuse to participate in flag salute ceremonies which violated the student's conscience.

Jones v. Opelika (1942); Murdock v. Pennsylvania (1943); Martin v. Struthers (1943); Watchtower v. Village of Stratton (2002)
These cases all dealt with door-to-door proselytizing and granted Jehovah's Witnesses the religious freedom to preach without a license or a permit and that town government cannot outlaw door-to-door visits.

Marsh v. Alabama (1946); Fowler v. Rhode Island (1953) and Krishna v. Lee (1992)
Marsh and *Fowler* gave Jehovah's Witnesses the right to distribute literature on the streets of a company town and to give an address in a public park. *Krisha* allowed members of the Krisha religion to distribute literature at airports.

McCollum v. Board of Education (1948)
The teaching of religious instruction in public schools was found to be unconstitutional.

Engel v. Vitale (1962); Abbington v. Schempp (1963); Tilton v Richardson(1971); Stone v. Graham 1980); Wallace v. Jaffree (1985); Newdow v. U.S. Congress (2002)
The following school activities were found to be unconstitutional: The saying of prayers; the reading of the Bible over the school intercom; the federal funding of private; religious and public colleges; the posting of the Ten Commandments; the enforcing of a moment of silence and the use of the words "under God" in the Pledge of Allegiance.

Cleveland v. United States (1946)
A woman cannot legally be transported across state lines to enter into a plural marriage even if doing so is motivated by religious belief.

Torcaso y. Watkins (1961)
Maryland cannot require applicants for public office to take an oath expressing a belief in the existence of God.

McMillan v. State (1970)
The Maryland Court of Appeals ruled that a lower court judge should not have held a person in contempt for refusing to remove a religious headgear while in court.

Lynch v. Donnelly (1984); Allegheny Co. v. ACLU (1989)
A government-owned nativity scene does not endorse religion and can be displayed on private land, but a nativity scene displayed inside a government building is in violation.

Employment Division v. Smith (1990); Church of Lukumi

Babalu Aye v. Hialeah (1993)

In *Employment*, it was held that no religious actions (the use of peyote, a hallucinogenic drug) may violate general laws, but that laws aimed specifically at a religion or a particular religious practice would be unconstitutional.

In *Church of Lukumi*, members of the Santeria religion were stopped from sacrificing animals (an illegal act), but were released from a local ordinance to prevent the sacrifices as the ordinance was aimed directly at the church.

Hate in the Name of God

Two media events this past year necessitate our reconsideration of the assumption that the permission of freedom of religion is always the "right thing to do." After the unsettling events of September 11, 2001, and the exposure of rampant sexual child abuse within the Catholic Church, we can no longer presume that religious expression could never harbor evil. News stories such as the following continue to give rise to the contemplation that our laws and the criminal justice system must work in harmony to prevent future violence to society perpetrated in the name of religious conscience.

From the *Adventist News Network Bulletin* of October 25, 2000, comes the report that "religious extremism is on the rise," according to a United Nations report. *The Washington Post* on August 17, 2002, reported that "Governor Jeb Bush told Muslim leaders the state will assess the safety of all Florida mosques and Islamic schools following the arrest of a doctor accused of plotting to blow up Islamic buildings." The Seventh Day Adventist Church, speaking from the international level addresses the following concerns:

> *...tragically some nations have published lists of religious groups described as potentially dangerous sects. Anti-sect commissions have been set up, investigative personnel have been trained and restrictive laws passed. Hundreds of thousands of innocent believers are now under official*

suspicion and are treated as second-class citizens. (Official Statement (1))

Various cult awareness movements expressed concern in 1999 after the Maryland Anti-Cult Resolution established a task force to look into religious cult activities at the University of Maryland. In a letter dated May 25, 1999, Nicholas P. Miller Esq., Executive Director of the Council on Religious Freedom, addressed the chairman of the task force stating:

It will be impossible for the Task Force to decide what groups are 'cults' without making value judgments with religious implications. The Council protests the formation and operation of this Task Force as an unconstitutional unwise decision that will allow any legitimate targets of the government's concern and inquiry to attain sympathy status as targets of a state initiated religious inquisition.

Conclusion

Back on September 19 of this year, the following spam appeared on my personal email. It was signed and is quoted here, complete with typographical errors and misspellings:

I am a student at WV Wesleyan College, and my major is Musical Education. Unfortunately, I have to take a Legal Aspects of Teaching course. I must inform everyone, as much as you and I may not like it, but prayer in school is extremely unconstitutional. Praying in school infringes upon the constitutional rights of people with alternative belief systems, be it Muslim, Hindu, Bhuddist, Pagan, Jewish, Jahova's Whitnesses, Athiest, etc.. There is no possible way to standardize prayer to accommodate every religion and every student. Most schools do have a moment of silence for individual prayer, but that is the closest that the constitution will allow. Separation of Church and State is a necessary evil, life would be more complicated for us if we allow the Church to rule our Government, i.e., Palestine, Israel. Thank you very much for your time; I mean no offence to any of you.

The writer instructed me to sign the "petition" and pass it on. The purpose of the petition remained unstated. Even so, 550 names were already on it. What is of utmost concern, however, is the recognition that religious conviction can sometimes be one of the strongest emotional turbulences within the human heart. It can be fanned to a dangerous degree, which may motivate violence against another. A mob-like spirit then erupts and intolerance rules rather than rationality. If "power corrupts", then power behind religious fervor can be corrupted to the point that reason is abandoned, and followers are incited to such actions as suicidal missions such as bombings and the flying of airplanes into occupied buildings. Conscience can also be hardened to the point that a deaf ear is turned from the cries of children sacrificed to gratifications of pedophiles. When this level of religious zeal exists, written laws are useless, as the law of the treacherous heart rules with senseless abandon.

This leaves each of us to decide within our own heart, as Daniel did, just what we will do when faced with the dilemma of determining our action, or non-action, in a situation demanding that we obey either God or the law.

IN THE CIRCUIT COURT FOR ANNE ARUNDEL COUNTY, MARYLAND

CHARITY COURTS DULANY
1234 Prestigious Naval Academy Drive
Annapolis, Maryland
      Plaintiff
vs
DANIEL, "THE ELDER", DULANY
1234 Prestigious Naval Academy Drive
Annapolis, Maryland
      Defendant

<u>COMPLAINT FOR AN ABSOLUTE DIVORCE</u>
Charity Courts Dulany, Plaintiff, by Judith L. Delaney and Delaney and Associates, her attorney, respectfully represents unto your Honor as follows:

1. That on April 10, 1710 she was married to Daniel, "the Elder" Dulany in Anne Arundel County in a religious ceremony.
2. That the Plaintiff and Defendant have been residents of the State of Maryland for more than one year immediately prior to the filing of this complaint.
3. That four children were born to the parties as a result of their marriage; namely, Loyd Dulany, born April 10, 1713, Daniel, "the Younger", Dulany, born June 22, 1722, Dennis Dulany, born April 10, 1726, and Walter Dulany, born April 10, 1730.
4. That Defendant did commit adultery. Plaintiff has neither forgiven nor condoned said conduct, and there is no reasonable hope or expectation of a reconciliation between the parties. On March 10, 1742, Promiscuity Tasker, the eighteen-year-old unmarried daughter of Benhaydad Tasker of Bowie, Maryland, gave birth to triplet daughters whom she named Danielle, Danette and Dannee Dulany. On March 15, 1742, Daniel, "the Elder" Dulany signed the attached Exhibit A entitled: "My Agreement to Financially Support My Three Minor Daughters

Born to Promiscuity Tasker".

5. That both Plaintiff and Defendant are residing at 1234 Prestigious Naval Academy Drive, Annapolis, Maryland which is owned by the parties, but in separate quarters of the house in separate bedrooms. Each Plaintiff and Defendant is being attended to by separate crews of domestic staff made up primarily of slaves, but managed by one Miss Tell-It-All Gossip, Headmistress, in the case of the crew attending the Plaintiff and one Grafton McGee, Head Butler, in the case of the crew attending the Defendant. Attached as Exhibit B is a "Statement of Tell-It-All Gossip" establishing that the Defendant has not paid a visit to the separate quarters or separate bedroom of the Plaintiff since March 10, 1742.

6. That both Loyd and Daniel, "the Younger", Dulany have reached majority and are emancipated. Dennis and Walter Dulany, minors, reside with their parents at the family residence.

7. That the parties have substantial real property acquired during their marriage and used primarily for family residence and investment purposes, including the Prestigious Naval Academy Drive property as well as some 20 mansions and unimproved land parcels located in Annapolis, Dulany Valley, Baltimore, Frederick and Western Maryland and Northern Virginia and some 200 slaves. All said property is titled in Defendant's name, but is due to pass to the Plaintiff under the terms of the Defendant's "Last Will and Testament" dated April 11, 1710.

8. That the parties have substantial personal property, some of which is titled in the joint names of the parties, and some of which is titled in the name of the Plaintiff or the Defendant separately.

9. That the minor child, Dennis, is presently a boarding school student in London and has expressed his desire to remain at school until graduation when he will have reached majority. The parties have agreed to joint custody of Dennis with equitable visitation rights to be agreed upon within 30 days.

10. That the minor child, Walter, is presently in the custody of the Plaintiff who the parties have agreed to be the fit and proper person to have custody. Equitable visitation rights on behalf of the Defendant are to be decided upon within 30 days.

11. That the Plaintiff has not participated as a party, witness or in any other capacity in any litigation concerning the custody of the minor children in this or any other state. The Plaintiff has no information or any custody proceedings concerning the children pending in a court of this or any other state. The only other person known to the Plaintiff who has a claim to the custody of the children or visitation rights is the Defendant.

WHEREFORE, the Plaintiff prays:

A. That she be awarded an absolute divorce from the Defendant.

B. That she be awarded joint custody of the minor, Walter, and

C. That she be awarded alimony and child support, pendente lite and permanent.

D. That the court pass a use and possession order permitting the Plaintiff and the minor child, Walter, to occupy the north wing of the family home until Walter reaches the age of majority on April 10, 1748.

E. That the court pass a use and possession order permitting the Plaintiff and the minor child, Walter, to have continued use of the family personal property now contained in the north wing of the family home until Walter reaches the age of majority on April 10, 1748. The Plaintiff is to provide a list of said personal property to the court within 30 days.

F. That the court pass an order accepting a lease between the parties and Thomas Jefferson regarding the family home to take effect on April 11, 1748, to lease the residence for a renewable ten-year term and providing that the rent be split equally between the parties until the lease shall not be renewed. At the time of the lease becoming null and void, the house shall be sold at market value and the proceeds of the sale shall be split equally between the parties.

G. That the court determine the ownership of all other real property and slave-holdings titled in the name of Daniel, the Elder, Dulany, excluding the family home mentioned above and order an appraisal of said properties and that the Plaintiff receive a sum equal to one-half the value of same.

H. That the court determine the ownership of all personal and marital properties titled in the names of both parties or either of them, excluding the personal clothing and jewelry belonging to the Plaintiff, and grant to the Plaintiff a monetary award as an adjustment of the personal and marital properties.

I. That the monetary award in "H" above be reduced to a judgment in favor of the Plaintiff.

J. That the Defendant be ordered to pay the Plaintiff reasonable counsel fees and the costs of these proceedings.

K. That the Plaintiff be awarded such other and further relief as the nature of her cause may require.

_____   _____

Charity Courts Dulany   Judith L. Delaney
                                 3860 Kenilworth Avenue
                                 Annapolis, Maryland

IN THE CIRCUIT COURT FOR ANNE ARUNDEL COUNTY, MARYLAND

CHARITY COURTS DULANY
Plaintiff and Cross-Defendant
vs
DANIEL, "THE ELDER", DULANY
Defendant and Cross-Plaintiff

ANSWER TO COMPLAINT FOR ABSOLUTE DIVORCE AND COUNTERCLAIM FOR ABSOLUTE DIVORCE AND OTHER RELIEF TO THE HONORABLE, THE JUDGE OF SAID COURT:

Daniel, "the Elder" Dulany, by Thomas Jefferson, his attorney, in answer to the Complaint filed against him, respectfully says:

1. He admits the allegations of Paragraphs 1, 2, and 3 of the Complaint.

2. He admits the allegations of Paragraph 4 with the exception that the Plaintiff has forgiven and condoned the Defendant's adultery with Promiscuity Tasker.

3. He admits the allegations of Paragraph 7 with the exception that the Defendant's "Last Will and Testament" is dated April 15, 1742, and devises and bequeaths his estate to be shared equally between his four sons, Loyd, Daniel, "the Younger", Dennis and Walter Delaney.

4. He denies the allegations of Paragraph 8 of the Complaint.

5. He admits the allegations of Paragraphs 9 and 10 of the Complaint.

6. Further answering, he avers that on April 15, 1742, the Plaintiff entered into the private quarters and bedroom of the Defendant and engaged in intercourse with the Defendant. The Defendant's Head Butler, Grafton McGee, unexpectedly entered the private quarters of the Defendant at approximately 10 p m on April 15, 1742, and is prepared to testify that he overheard conversation in which the Plaintiff

forgave the Defendant as they conversed in the marital bed and also, upon her leaving the quarters, he overheard the Plaintiff confess to adultery with one Crazyman Calvert.

WHEREFORE, Defendant requests that the Complaint be dismissed with costs to be paid by the Plaintiff.

COUNTERCLAIM FOR ABSOLUTE DIVORCE AND OTHER RELIEF

Daniel, "the Elder", Dulany, Counter-Plaintiff by his attorney, Thomas Jefferson, respectfully represents unto your Honor:

1. That on April 10, 1710, he was married to Charity Courts Dulany in Anne Arundel County in a religious ceremony.

2. That the Plaintiff and Defendants have been residents of the State of Maryland for more than one year immediately prior to the filing of this Complaint.

3. That four children were born to the parties as a result of their marriage, namely Loyd Dulany, born April 10, 1713; Daniel, "the Younger" Dulany, born June 22, 1722; Dennis Dulany, born April 10, 1726; and Walter Dulany, born April 10, 1730. Loyd and Daniel, "the Younger" have both reached majority and are emancipated. Custody and visitation rights for the two minors, Dennis and Walter, have been worked out by the parties and are set out in attached Exhibit AA.

4. That the Counter-Defendant did commit adultery and Counter-Plaintiff has neither forgiven or condoned said conduct, and there is no reasonable hope of a reconciliation between the parties.

WHEREFORE, the Counter-Plaintiff requests:

1. That he be awarded an absolute divorce from the Counter-Plaintiff.

2. That the court pass an order accepting the custody, visitation rights, alimony, and child support as set out in Exhibit A.

3. That the court pass an order distributing the marital property as set out in Exhibit B entitled "Distribution of Marital Property and the Sharing of the Family Home" signed by both parties.

4. That the court pass an order accepting the "Lease" to Mr. Thomas Jefferson of the family home signed by both parties and Mr. Jefferson.

5. That the Counter-Defendant be ordered to pay Counter-Plaintiff's reasonable counsel fees and the cost of these proceedings.

6. That the Counter-Plaintiff be awarded such other and further relief as the nature of his cause may require.

_____   _____
Daniel "the Elder" Dulany   Thomas Jefferson
                                  2222 Independence Avenue
                                  Annapolis, Maryland

CERTIFICATE OF SERVICE
I HEREBY CERTIFY that on this April 20, 1742, I mailed a copy of the foregoing Answer and Counter-Complaint to Judith L. Delaney, to her office at 3860 Kenilworth Avenue, Annapolis, Maryland

_____
Thomas Jefferson

IN THE CIRCUIT COURT FOR ANNE ARUNDEL COUNTY, MARYLAND

CHARITY COURTS DULANY
Plaintiff and Cross-Defendant
vs
DANIEL "THE ELDER" DULANY
Defendant and Cross-Plaintiff

ANSWER TO COUNTERCLAIM FOR ABSOLUTE DIVORCE

Charity Courts Dulany, Plaintiff and Cross-Defendant, by Judith L. Delaney and Delaney and Associates, her attorney, in Answer to the Counterclaim for an Absolute Divorce filed herein states as follows:

   1. She admits the allegations contained in 1, 2, 3 and 4 of the Counterclaim.

WHEREFORE, the Plaintiff and Cross-Defendant having fully answered the Complaint prays:

That the court grants the Absolute Divorce and all the other requests of the Defendant and Cross-Plaintiff as outlined in the Counterclaim.

_____   _____
Charity Courts Dulany   Judith L. Delaney
                                   3860 Kenilworth Avenue
                                   Annapolis, Maryland

CERTIFICATE OF SERVICE

I HEREBY CERTIFY on this 25th day of April 1742, that I mailed a copy of the aforegoing Answer to Thomas Jefferson, Esquire, at 2222 Independence Avenue, Annapolis, Maryland.

_____
Judith L. Delaney

7
The First Dulany Story

According to my online research and some family research done by the Delaneys,

Basil Delaney's family arrived in Maryland in 1703. Daniel Dulany, along with two older brothers, left Ireland indentured to the captain of the ship, having lost the financial support of their father, Thomas, due to a rift with his second wife. Thomas and his new wife, along with their family, arrived in 1709 and settled in Maryland. Basil's family descended from this second family, which settled in southern Maryland and became farmers, schoolteachers, business owners, and such. Some then moved to Pennsylvania and then south into West Virginia, where Basil was born in 1947. Daniel Dulany, the Elder, was born in 1685 in Ireland and became a prominent lawyer and land developer in colonial Maryland, holding several colonial offices. He was indentured to Colonel George Plater II for a three-year period as a law clerk, after which he returned to London to study law. He was admitted to the Charles County Bar in 1709. He was elected to represent the town of Annapolis in the General Assembly. In 1722, he wrote a pamphlet asserting the rights of Marylanders to the benefits of English laws. He became wealthy, accumulated land, and is credited with founding the city of Frederick, Maryland. At his death in 1753, it was said he owned 47,000 acres of land.

Daniel Dulany, the Younger, was born in Annapolis in 1722 and was educated in England. He was the Mayor of Annapolis. Fellow lawyer and politician, William Pinkney, regarded him as the peer of any lawyer in America or England, declaring that "even among such men as Fox, Pitt, and Sheridan, he had not found his superior."

Daniel, the Elder, and Daniel, the Younger, were both prominent in defining Maryland's founding principles and had strong legal and political influences on the colony. Aubrey C. Land published a historical book about the family entitled *The Dulanys of Maryland* in 1955. The younger Daniel would surpass his father's outstanding legal reputation to become the most highly regarded attorney in Maryland. Although he refused to support the overthrow of British rule in Maryland, he notably opposed the Stamp Act of 1765.

He wrote the important 55-page pamphlet entitled "Considerations on the Propriety of Imposing Taxes on the British Colonies, For the Purpose of Raising a Revenue by Act of Parliament," which argued against taxation without representation.

An example of Dulany's writing style can be found on page 14 of the pamphlet, where he makes a comparison and says, "as it would be to call Lake Erie a duck puddle because it is not the Atlantic Ocean." The use of the term "taxation without representation" used in the pamphlet would become the slogan summarizing the colonial grievances, which led to the Revolutionary War and independence, which was not the intention of the author.

When the war came, Daniel, the Younger, remained a Loyalist and most of his substantial property was confiscated in 1781.

The Dulany story is particularly interesting in that it truly represents what many immigrants call the "American Dream." Daniel, the Elder, arrived in the colonies at the age of 18. The young man was financially destitute and entered voluntarily into an arrangement of indentured servitude. This was popular in the United States in the 1600s, when many European immigrants worked without pay in exchange for the price of their passage to America. However, he would rise to wealth as well as prominence in the fields of law, business, and politics. His son would follow in his footsteps.

Daniel, the Elder, whose religion was Anglican, married Rebecca Smith, the daughter of Col. Walter Smith, with whom he had seven children. After her death, he married Henrietta Maria Lloyd Chew, with whom he had two children. His house was built on the present grounds of the U.S. Naval Academy. He is interred in St. Anne's Churchyard, Annapolis, Maryland.

Daniel, the Younger, married Rebecca Tasker, daughter of Benjamin Tasker of Maryland. They had four children. Benjamin Tasker Dulany served in the Revolutionary War as an aide to George Washington, having married Washington's goddaughter, Elizabeth French. Daniel, the Younger, died in Baltimore in 1797 and was buried in St. Paul's Cemetery.

Daniel Dulany, The Elder 1685-1753

Daniel Dulany, The Younger 1722-1797

8

The Thompson Story

Hugh and his Hunting Dog

My Father Used to Say …

Judith Delaney
English 102H, #9820
JE# 5, October 1, 2001

My father, Harold H. Thompson, of Philippi, West Virginia, was diagnosed two years ago with prostate cancer. His team of doctors at the VA Hospital concluded after numerous tests and consultations that my dad was not a candidate for either surgery or chemotherapy. His cancer was already in its final stages, and although drugs could slow it down, it would eventually take his life. I started to actively grieve. I say "actively" because I believe I subconsciously anticipated his death in my earliest childhood due to his addiction and risky behavior. So, I have waited, along with him, for the past 50 years for him to, as he would say, "give it up."

You see, my father, as my psychiatrist once told me, "Stepped off the boat walking dead" in 1945 when he returned to America after fighting Germans in Italy. He once told me he, by necessity, took a civilian life when he forced an old Italian man and his donkey to step off the road. He had orders not to move his vehicle (which was loaded with gasoline supplies) off the road because landmines had been planted by the Germans to harm Allied troops traveling the road. He described it as a horrible experience for him. He went into the town and made a report. The man's family came to the scene.

Daddy's untreated post-traumatic stress disorder embarked him on a long, painful road of depression, alcoholism, suicidal ideologies, and emotional turmoil which will rage through the minds of my mother, his children, and their children. My psychiatrist diagnosed me with post-traumatic stress disorder from my exposure to him from my infancy.

I believe I'm one of the very few surviving people whose lives he has touched who would stand up and say: "I really loved that man." Do I understand him? No, he's too simple and too complex to truly be understood. Do I forgive him? Yes! He's my hero because he takes responsibility for his weaknesses and he says, "I'm sorry." Will I miss him? With all my heart, I will. Although I've already begun to grieve, it may take the rest of my life to complete it. I do have hope. I know Jesus likened death to sleep. Sleeping people wake up, and I expect my dad to wake up in the resurrection.

I value every minute I talk to him or see him now. This is a good time to write down some of the things he has said to me over the years. After he's sleeping, I'll find this incomplete list useful as I reflect on some of the things my father used to say:

- "I had to make a tough decision the other day. I didn't have enough money to pay for both my truck insurance and my new dentures. I thought it over—you don't need teeth to drink beer. I paid for the insurance."
- "If you don't like my gate, don't swing on it."
- "When your mother had the twins, I wanted to name them John and Quit, but she wouldn't stand for that. We already had four kids, we went on and had two more after the twins, eight in all."
- "I told you kids not to marry an Italian born in Italy; you might be related."
- "A cop was following me down the road, and I was driving drunk, so I pulled off the road and started walking, he arrested me for drunk walking."
- "Don't stir a bucket of poop, it will stink more."
- "If you let a bird build a nest in your hair, it's your fault."
- "I heard this guy trying to sell someone a security storm

door for $1,000, I told him I once bought a farm for $400."

- "I had a '39 Ford coupe when I went into the Army, and I didn't want anyone driving it while I was gone. I took it out by the woods and parked it and took the key with me. I went out there the other day, and that old car was still there, all rusted out, even had a tree growing right through it. I guess no one will drive it now."
- "I told your mother just the other day that since you kids are all grown up, I'd like to adopt a baby. I like girls, they're so cute. I think I will adopt a girl, about 19 years old."
- "Did I ever tell you about the time my brother, June, and I decided to jump a freight train to go up to Belington to see some girls? He jumped up in the car first, but I missed. So, I jumped in the car right behind him—it didn't have a floor in it—I ran all the way to Belington."
- "Why do you ask me if I've been drinking, I'll just say: 'the possibility is involved.'"
- "Now, I told all my sons-in-law they had to pay for you girls. I spent all my money raising you. One of them said he would just send her back and get a refund. Your husband hasn't even made an installment payment, maybe I'll have to repossess you."
- "I cleared a little bit of land off near the meadow and told your sister I wanted to get a pony for the grandchildren to ride when they come in. She told me all my grandchildren have driver's licenses, but maybe the great-grandchildren would like to ride a pony."
- "That girl of your sister is always coming in here to devil me. She tries to tickle me. So, I told her I was going to knock her down a rat hole and put a brick on it. She said: 'Grandpa, you can't lift a brick!'"
- "I was thinking the other day about the war. They said it was self-defense. I don't get it. I got on a boat and spent

days, maybe weeks, I don't remember, but it took a long time to cross the ocean, so how was it self-defense if I went there?"

- "If there is another war, I'll not go. I wouldn't give a million dollars for the experience, but they can shoot me. I won't go."
- "When I die, I'm too crooked for them to bury me, they'll have to screw me in the ground."
- "You told me when we went over to the VA Hospital to talk to the doctors that I should look for the good news and the bad news. The good news is I have cancer, the bad news is I'm gonna live."

Some Memories of My Brother, Hugh

Written the day after Hugh's death on April 11, 2002

I remember the time Hugh traded for a Model T Ford car. Hugh wasn't very old at the time. The Model T did not have a gear shift. It had three pedals. When the left pedal was pushed, the car was in low gear. Release the same pedal, and the car was in high gear. The center pedal was reverse when pushed in and held in. The pedal to the right was the brake. The gas throttle was located on the steering column. Pull down on the lever to accelerate. The same type of lever on the left side of the steering column was for spark. There was no self-starter. It had a crank located on the front to start the engine. After the engine started by cranking, a switch turned to the left to place it on magnets. The magnets acted as a battery. There was no floorboard in the car, which there should have been. The exhaust pipes would get hot, and I was barefoot. At times I would burn my feet on the exhaust pipes.

The reverse system was worn out. When we wanted to turn around, William and I would get out of the car and push it backward. We really had fun on the back dirt roads with that car. As well as I remember, we took it to a neighbor's woods and let it sit. In other words, we junked it.

Hugh liked to rabbit hunt in his younger days when we were children. He usually had a rabbit dog. He also liked to squirrel hunt.

He also did these things in his adulthood.

Hugh liked sports also. Baseball was his greatest sport. He was at a baseball game with his girlfriend at Mt. Liberty. He wasn't on the team. The manager noticed him on the sideline and asked him to pinch hit. Hugh went in the game as a pinch hitter and knocked a home run.

He entered the Army during World War II, on December 28, 1942. He was in the European theater. He was in those battles from North Africa through Italy until VE Day, May 8, 1945.

I also had another brother in the same area, Gearl Thompson. They tried very hard to locate each other but did not do so. After they returned home, they were talking about their experiences. At one time, they were within seven miles of each other.

When Hugh wrote letters home, he would try to give us a clue as to where he was located overseas. The mail was censored. Hugh said, "I am glad to hear our niece, Shirley Ruth, is in the fifth grade. Why did you cut the maple tree in the yard?" That meant he was in Naples, Italy, with the Fifth Army. Shirley Ruth wasn't even in school yet, but the fifth grade meaning the Fifth Army and the maple tree referring to Naples, Italy. We didn't even have a maple tree in our yard. He was in the Heavy Field Artillery 985th. Our brother, Gearl, was in the 21st Engineers Corp. Hugh was in several major battles.

After he returned home, he married Mavis Corley. They had eight children—Janet, Judy, Gary, Cindy, Chris, Cathy, David, and Donnie. He did mechanic work and farming. He worked at different garages in Philippi and Belington: Haddix Garage, Kines Motor, and Raymond Wilmoth's garage. He also worked as a welder for Badger Coal Company. Hugh and June were considered "top" mechanics in Barbour County.

Hugh will be greatly missed in his family, in the community and by all who knew him. We all will miss you.

Your brother,

Bob

Transcript of Interview by Gary Thompson of His Father, Hugh, and His Uncle Bob on July 8-9, 1994

Note: Some names have been changed.

July 8, 1994

GARY: Dad. who's the oldest? I guess you are. Where were you born? Where were you guys living when you were born?

HUGH: I forget ... I think it was up at Grandpa Thompson's, wasn't it? Grandpa and Grandma Thompson's house. Mom and Dad rented that. I think I was born at the old place, right on this side of the old home place. I don't know. I forget, but I do remember, you know this big house on the right, someone built right on top of the hill. I used to own that land. I remember when we lived there. I couldn't have been over three or four years old. I don't think Bob was born yet. We had a grate, and me and Mom, she went in and built a fire in the grate, and she came in. She had a fur coat, well, it wasn't a fur coat, but it looked like fur, probably artificial, and hung it on the back of the chair. Well, I was poking in the fire, and after a while, the poker got red hot clear up to there, so I turned around, some way or another, and got her coat on fire! So, buddy, I'm tellin' you, I hated that. It burned every bit of it. So, I put the poker up beside the, you know, the fireplace.

GARY: What did Grandma do?

HUGH: She screamed, and she hollered, but she never whipped one of us boys, as I ever remember. My dad, now buddy, he'd put it on you. But I don't remember my mother ever whippin' any of us boys. You know, a few days, a few weeks before she died, I was up there and I said: "Mom, how many boys you got?"

She said: "Five."

I said: "I'm the third one down."

She said: "Yeah."

I said: "Was I the orneriest one in the bunch?"

She said: "I think so!" And she just grinned!

She was at the hospital in Elkins, and I asked her: "Mom, you want to go back home?"

She said: "Yeah, I want to go back to the Good Samaritan. They treat you good there."

Well, I don't know whether I'm going to go there. I might go to Washington, DC, to the Old Soldier's Home.

GARY: No, you're going to Alaska!

HUGH: Maybe someday

GARY: We'll get you up in Alaska, and you won't be able to leave because you must get on an airplane to leave, so …

HUGH: … airplanes? That's left up to the boss, my wife.

GARY: I keep telling him he needs to spend the hottest part of West Virginia in Alaska, then go to Hawaii in the winter. He doesn't seem to want to leave West Virginia for some reason.

HUGH: Bob, I'm telling you the truth, we had a good time down in Honolulu. Janet bought me three shirts, and we went clear from one end to the other. We were in Honolulu. They live in Honolulu. They live in Honolulu …

GARY: They live right out of Honolulu … about 30 miles, I think Janet said.

HUGH: We seen that big cemetery … we got pictures of the National Cemetery

GARY: Do you remember Pop? When I was a kid, they talked about Pop a lot, but I don't remember him? I remember Pap Pap real well.

HUGH: We used to go out there ... well, we were cuttin' filth over the hill, John Green was helpin' cut it. We tried to clean up a place over there. Well, we did get a place cleaned up, and we put it in potatoes. And we'd go in every noon, at noon; we'd eat a big supper. Dad, Mom, and them would have a big supper, and Grandma Ella. Pop would take us up there. We'd have to take turns turning this here crank to turn the grindstone to sharpen the scythes. He was something else.

GARY: Did he have horses? I think I remember that.

HUGH: Oh yeah, he had Pat and Old ... one we called Bill. Dad doubled up with him one time, and her name was Pat. She was a white horse, and Old Bill was a black one. I never did like that Old Bill. Me and Gearl would be a'plowin' over there, we rented a piece of corn field from Raymond Fridley. I would drive a little bit, and Gearl would drive a little bit, and I'd plow a little bit. I wasn't very big. We'd get to the end of the turn, and we'd have to click the lever on the plow, raise it up in the air, it automatically turns, you see, then turn the same furrow. It wasn't a land side, it was a hillside. I remember one-time, Old Pat, she done all the work. She was way ahead all the time, and Old Bill was always laggin' behind. I shouldn't a'did this, but I got me a sassafras switch about that long, and I put a needle, or one of those straight pins, in it. When I was drivin', every time he'd start laggin' behind, going half way to sleep, I'd punch him! Right in the rear, you know! Boy! He'd get up there! Well, after about two or three minutes, we'd get clear across the field, and he'd get behind. I'd hit him again! I'll never forget. I always hated that horse; I don't know why. Pop had an old log barn up there and he'd raise homemade tobacco. Well, I'd slip out there and he had put his tobacco up there in the barn, hung it up there. Big leaves, about that long. I'd get me two or three and I'd take it home. I'd wind it up like that and run it through Mom's sieve, and then I'd roll 'em. I didn't care what kind of paper it was, newspaper or anything … it's a wonder I hadn't died, but I rolled cigarettes.

GARY: How old were you then?

HUGH: I couldn't be over five or six. I smoked ever since … I smoked 66 years!

GARY: You don't deserve to be alive today!

HUGH: You know, sometimes I wonder about that. Why in the heck am I still livin'?

GARY: Same reason that Grandma said, you were the ornery one, probably! Too ornery to die! … So, he kept his tobacco out in the barn, huh?

HUGH: I would steal a couple of leaves every day and smoke in the barn.

GARY: He was ornery, wasn't he?

BOB: I think Mom was right.

HUGH: I always liked to smoke. I don't know why. I would steal out two eggs a day off Grandma and Grandpa Thompson, and we had some chickens, and I'd steal up a couple there, and in about five or six days, I had a dozen eggs, and I'd go down to the old country store, remember it, Bob? I'd go in there and get me a pack of RJR.

GARY: That tobacco?

HUGH: Uh-huh. Had a little drawstring on top. RJR. So, I had a little bag of that RJR, and I was goin' to school up there. I don't know how old I was. Marlene Andrick, no, not Marlene … what was that woman's name? I told her …

BOB: Miss Ella England.

HUGH: Miss England. We was up under the school house, had a hole in the school house bottom where you could go back under the floor and smoke. One of 'em, Dottie Wilmoth, or Laura Ann Price, … came in and said: "Hey. Hugh, you better put that cigarette out. Here comes Miss England." And I thought she was kiddin'!

I said: "The heck with Miss England! If she fools with me, I'll knock
   her on her head!"

I looked back there, and there she was standin' there! Well, I wasn't
   about to go back in that building. It was noon hour. So, I took
   off and came over through Bill Wright's hill, and Herbert Williams and Mabel lived up there on old Donald Poling's place. I
   kept asking Mabel every once and a while: "What time is it?
   What time is it?" Well, I knew for a fact that I was goin' to get a
   trimmin', and I figured—"Now, if I wait long enough until Bob
   and William and Gearl and them get out of school, I'll go in, and
   I'll meet 'em down there and I'll walk in. Maybe they don't know
   I skipped school!" Oh, boy! That didn't work. Boy! I got it then.

GARY: So how did they find out?

HUGH: I forget exactly. Do you remember, Bob?

BOB: Oh, I was the one who told 'em!

HUGH: The funniest thing about it, me and him and William were
   going to school up there ... oh, yeah! ... and Anna May Daughtery,
   she was the principal. So, I finally went back to school the next
   day, and I put 'bout three or four pairs of pants on, and I put a
   big pasteboard in my britches and walked in there. Anna May
   Daughtery said: "Everyone's excused but Hugh, I want to talk to
   him." Well, they went out, and I was sittin' there. Oh, boy! She told
   me off! Then I thought, "Well, boy, this is my punishment." Well,
   the next day, I went to school, and I didn't have those pants on,
   and Miss Daughtery said: "Everyone's excused but Hugh. Miss
   England wants to see him in the other room." And I went in
   there, and I'm tellin' you, she had a paddle that long, big holes
   bored in it, and she turned me across her knee. Oh, man! I'm
   tellin' you. That hurt! They's the ones told 'em I had two or three
   pairs of pants on 'cause I was expectin' a whippin', ya know. Well,
   those were the good old days, weren't they?

GARY: How old were you when you got the whippin' for that?

HUGH: Well, I was in the big room. Fourth grade went in the big
   room.

BOB: Fifth.

HUGH: Fifth. I must have been in the fifth or sixth. I was pretty big by then, wasn't I? I was big enough to know better.

GARY: What school was that? Was that over at Point Pleasant?

HUGH: Point Pleasant. I'll never forget the time Shorty Poe, remember "Old Shorty"?

Big, tall, ya know, and I was sittin', this was in the small room, I was sittin in about the fourth seat, and "old Shorty," you know him, we used to play ball?

GARY: Little League?

HUGH: He was your coach. He had the job of janitor, taking care of the stove, keeping the place heated, he's sweep it out and dust off. He came in there and said: "Hugh, come here." I said: "No, I can't." "No, come on." I jumped out of my seat and started back there to see what he was going to say, and it didn't go too good! ... You know my first teacher? At Mt. Liberty? Can you remember us when we lived at Jake Jones' place?

We'd walk across the hill ... well, maybe you didn't Bob. But I did. Doris Griffith and me and William. I don't think he was old enough yet. Anyway, Doris Griffith gave me my first whippin'. Fox Marsh gave me one at Union.

GARY: Sounds like you got a lot of 'em! I mean your first whippin', you said that was your first teacher, so that was your first year in school, right?

HUGH: Yeah, I was in first grade ... and Bart Malcolm, now he was sittin' here, and he was pretty good back in those days, by heck, he was about 15 or 16 years old and still in grade school ... I don't know how old he was, anyway, Doris. ... someone knocked on the door, the schoolhouse door, and she went to the door, opened up, and she was talkin' to this person. I don't remember who it was, but she came back, and Bart had us all a'laughin'. And I'm tellin' you the truth, I felt sorry for Bart. Doris went up there and got some switches and started beatin' him over the back. He only had a little old shirt on, and he wouldn't cry. Doris Griffith said: "I'll whip you til you do cry!" By heck, Bart never did cry. I bet you she whipped him five or six times. I always felt sorry for him for that ... old Doris Griffith. I guess she was my first schoolteacher at Mt. Liberty. I remember I was in the first grade, is that what you call the "primer"? Anyway, I done something wrong, and she said: "Now everyone's going on a picnic, and a hike, a walk, except Hugh." She made me sit there in that little seat by myself! I forgot what I did, but evidently, she didn't like it.

GARY: That was Mt. Liberty? You first went to school at Mt. Liberty?

HUGH: Mt. Liberty, then I went to Valley Dell two or three times, no two times, Point Pleasant once. I guess. But when I went to Valley Dell down there, I was just a little fellow. We'd walk over the hill here, and Madge Fisher, June's wife, and Susie Anzell, down there. Well, anyway, Larry Poling was teaching school, and he was at the blackboard, and I was doing something like that, and I was sittin' right behind Madge and Susie Anzell, and I was punching 'em or something. He turned around and seen me. "Hey!" At that time some of the seats were about that wide. "You like them girls?" I said: "Why not?" He said: "How would you like to sit with 'em?" I said: "Ah, I don't like that." He said: "You get up there!" He made me sit between my sister-in-law (wasn't my sister-in-law then) and Susie Anzell! Ah, man! Hey, it's his turn!

GARY: Bob, what do you remember about all these rotten things the old man did?

BOB (laughing): I remember a little bit about it. Of course, Hugh was talking about the old home place, the Jones' place, that was the place over there where Daughterys used to live. The old house that burned.

GARY: Yeah.

BOB: Dad built that house there. Dad owned all that in there.

GARY: I can just barely remember that. Wasn't there a fence around that? Out by the barn? We built the pond, and then there was a barn, it was kinda over in here.

BOB: But the house burned down. Adam Daughtery came up there and built another house. But the old house had burned down. Dad built it and dug that big well out there in the front, too. I just remember living there. I was only about four years old. We moved from up there to where we live now, to where the old house is now. I think I was four years old when we moved from over here to where Dad built the other house. I just barely remember. I think it was 1932, or 1930, 1931, or '32. Dad built that house up there, didn't he? If it was '32, I must have been six years old.

HUGH: I wasn't very big. I helped Dad build that. I remember.

BOB: I remember living over there, just barely remember.

HUGH: Do you remember when we dug that well? We got across the hollow, there's a wet weather spring over there, we'd get water over there till Dad started diggin' that well. It's still over there. Locked up.

BOB: Yeah, I know that well's still there, but I don't remember when we dug it.

HUGH: I remember when we were living there, and the place burned down. I remember when we dug the well at the last home place. I was just 10 years old. Dad and I drilled a hole. I got out and Dad set the charge. He started up the ladder … there was a fuse about that long, black powder is what it was. He lit the fuse, and he started up the ladder, and he fell back down, and oh, my gosh, when he got to the top that thing went off, and I'm tellin' you, there were big stones that big around. Rocks flew out and hit the roof. We had to patch the roof. It's a wonder he hadn't got killed.

BOB: That's the house we lived in up there, the other place.

GARY: Up at Mt. Liberty?

BOB: Yeah.

HUGH: Dad was good at that. He helped wall that well up over there where Tom Burner lives now. It's only about that big around. Pop and Dad, they'd go down there, and they would be down there 10 to 15 minutes, and then they would have to come back out to get air, there was "black damp" (methane gas) there.

They'd take turns. They were only allowed in there for so long cause there was no air.

GARY: Where did you go to school first, Bob?

BOB: Point Pleasant was my first school.

GARY: Now did they just not build one at Mt. Liberty and Valley Dell?

BOB: They were there, but the reason, I guess, I always heard that the reason we had to go to Point Pleasant when we lived at the old home place is because that is in Barker District. Mt. Liberty and Valley Dell are in Philippi District. That was the reason, 'cause the last year that I went to Point Pleasant, the school bus was going by my house, and I could have rode to Mt. Liberty or Valley Dell either one, but I wasn't allowed to because it was in Philippi District, and I had to walk to Point Pleasant. Of course, I was glad of that because I didn't want to change schools anyhow. I would rather have walked to Point Pleasant than I would have changed schools. When it comes to changing schools, it's a little hesitant in getting acquainted, you know, and you feel inferior to other people, and I mean I've known families even in my teaching, families that were moving from house to house, maybe three or four times a year. This is not good for the children that are attending school because one school isn't carried on in the same individual way as the other school. But we had to move a couple of times because we had to move down to Grandma Daughtery's a couple of times to take care of her, and then that put us in Union School. I always wished I was back in Point Pleasant, you see, my old home school. It does make a difference to kids growing up, in changing schools so often, because it's hard for them to get adjusted. Well, how would you like to change jobs every six weeks? You see what I mean? Going on a new job is hard for you to get on to. It's just hard to get adjusted. Now I was born down at Edith Sencil's in the Union area, in an old store building, on Edith Sencil's side of the road, right across from where Bob Andrick lives, in the old Roy Jones' place.

GARY: Is that right in a turn down there?

BOB: Right at the foot of the hill below Tom Phillips'. It was on one of the sides there, and I think we must have lived there a couple of times. William was born there also. There's where we were born, and then, I guess we moved up to where Dad built the house over there … yeah, we were down there in 1935.

HUGH: I think I went to school at Union when we lived at Jacob Hartlaub's place.

BOB: Well, you did. Jacob Hartlaub moved to Brownton one year. They rented their house to Dad and Mom. You and Gearl and June went to Union that time.

GARY: Bob, do you remember Pop?

BOB: Oh, yeah. I remember Pop real well. Pop was just 60 years old when I was born. I remember he would get out there and help us hoe corn. I remember one time when we were working hoeing corn, we were hoeing corn for Raymond Fridley, on the farm there. We were way back around the hill, there, next to the Mouse Run Road, hoeing corn. Oh! It was hot! And that evening when we came in for supper, we ate at Raymond's, and my Grandpa Thompson was so tired and crampy, he was just too tired to eat. So, at that time, I must have been about 10 years old, he would have been 70 years old, see, out there hoeing corn in that hot sun all day at 70 years old. I'll never forget that. Another time, I remember, we had a big field over there where it is growing up now, in wheat, and Raymond and Louise Fridley had moved up here on the hill from over on the Middle Fork River. So, we all decided, Raymond and Louise wanted everybody to go over there on the 4th of July. So, we had no way to go other than they hired Jack Marsh, Gilbert's boy, to take them over there on the truck. Well, Gilbert said that each man that went, or each boy that was big enough to work, old enough to work, either had to give him a dollar or cut crops one day, the whole day. So, I remember that Dad said: "Well, we'll go if the wheat is cut." As well as I remember, Brance Thompson was cradling John Green and Raymond. And I knew that we were going to go swimming in the river over there, and I didn't have a bathing suit. So, I took an old sweater and made me a bathing suit. I was afraid that somebody else would get a hold of that bathing suit when we went over there the next day on the 4th of July, and take it, and I wouldn't get to use it! And I wore that thing all day in that wheat field, as hot as it was, with my clothes over top of it!

HUGH: We were binding wheat.

BOB: I was afraid somebody would get that bathing suit and, when I came in that evening, started to pull that off where that old fuzz and stuff was on that sweater, it stuck to me! But we did get to go to the Middle Fork River because we got the wheat out. So, the next day, Fred came along with his truck, and Raymond and Louise went, Grandma and Grandpa Thompson went, Edmund and Winnie, and Dale and Roma, Herbert and Mabel Williams, Dad and Mom and all of us boys, five of us. So that was a pretty good load! It was raining, and we rode the back of that truck, big ton truck all the way to Middle Fork. Then we had a flat tire! And they had to stop and change that tire. That must have took an hour to change the truck tire. I think it was on the way back. Maybe, on the inside, too. It had the dual wheels. Had to stop and change that tire. By the time we go over there, I don't know what time it was, but they spread their lunch out there on the ground someplace, and we all ate. Then we went to the river. Me and my little bathing suit! I remember Densel, though, he was about my size. He didn't have a bathing suit. They made him go naked, and they pulled him up out of the water. Didn't make Densel mad after he was swimming a while!

GARY: Denzel was Edmund's son?

BOB: Yeah. Hugh's speaking of cutting brush and filth back there with the scythes. We had the whole farm cleaned up with scythes. There wasn't any brush on it whatsoever, only maybe just a few trees around where there might have been a little woodland. Now it's hard to even get a jack rabbit to get through. But we used to raise wheat and corn and everything in there every year … yes, Fisher's had the mill down there. Herman

Fisher ground the wheat and corn, and Herman wouldn't even shut down for lunch. He ate breakfast and supper when he was grinding at the mill. He skipped lunch; he'd grind all day. I have seen wagons and horses lined up almost halfway up to Isaac Everson's waiting to get their wheat ground. He never charged any money for doing this. What he did was if you took a bushel of wheat to have ground into flour, he'd take a couple of gallons out of it for his toll. Then the day would come when he was up with his custom grinding, he would grind this for himself, and then he would sell the flour and corn mill to people that didn't have it, didn't raise wheat. And if you would go there, Gary, and didn't have the money to buy a sack of flour, you couldn't buy it from him, he wouldn't charge it to you. No way! Flour was about 65 cents a bag from what I can remember. But what he would do, he would say: "You go over to the house, and Dora will give you 65 cents, and come back over here and give it to me, and then you can have the flour." But you see what he was doing; he didn't want to fool with those books. Now that was Herman's idea of not fooling with books and records. And when you paid back, you had to take the money back over to the house and give Dora the 65 cents. You see, he was finished with it, he was clear of it. So, if any losers came along, why he was still in the clear, but Dora would be the loser! But I don't think very many people ever took advantage of them. I remember I heard Mom say one time that we were out of wheat. Didn't have any flour and probably didn't have any money. And she said Bruce Mitchell had been at the mill and had some wheat ground, and he found out something about this, and Bruce, when he took his flour, he left a bag of flour for the Thompson family. Now things were rough then. If you had a dime in your pocket or a quarter, or a 50-cent piece, that looked as big around as a wagon wheel … things were cheap, you could buy soup beans for $4 a hundred pounds but getting the $4! Dad worked on WPA, what they called the Works Progress Administration, during the Depression, it was under Roosevelt, for

$17.60 every two weeks; $35.20 a month. He worked three days a week, and then another group came in and worked three days a week. Every two weeks you got a check for $17.60 and that came by mail. The foreman didn't pay you on payday at the job site, it came by mail. And here we would sit waiting for that check, and if the check didn't come, we couldn't go get some groceries. I remember we had to make a trip to Belington one time. The check didn't come, and we went to the Belington Post Office—we were on the Belington route at the time—and asked if the check was in. And the clerk at the post office wouldn't hand that check over to us! It was there, and he said: "You'll have to go up and get the mail carrier, Mr. Smith, to come down here to this post office, and he'll issue the check." We had to make a trip to Laurel Mountain Road to get him to come down and give us that check. The postmaster would not hand us that check! For what reason, I don't know, maybe he already had his mail put up in a certain area for the next day's run, and he didn't want to mess with it. But the postmaster can do anything, he's in charge. He should have gone back there and given us that check. We shouldn't have had to run to Laurel Mountain Road to get the mail carrier to come down there to give us that check!

GARY: How did you get up there? Did you have a car?

BOB: Well, we had an old car, a '30 Chevrolet, and we were lucky enough that we had the money to put two gallons of gasoline in it to go. 'Course, gasoline was cheap at that time, you could buy five gallons for a dollar. Oil was 10 or 15 cents a quart. Tires were $8 or $9 a piece. But, still, that came hard.

HUGH: Do you remember when Charlie Bennett used to deliver mail on a horse? He'd ride a horse clear from Point Pleasant to Mt. Liberty. He'd carry a big box from Aunt Gladys—toys and clothes and shoes. He'd go down through and come up by Wagner's place and through Mt. Liberty and back by our place.

BOB: Yeah, he'd come down across, through East Bend and down the old road and come down at Mt. Liberty. Then he'd come out by our house and over to Green's. Then he'd come out over at Knapp's garage. But, as I said, times were rough. I remember one time when I started to high school. I needed a pair of gym shoes, they were for a gym course, and I didn't have any money. The shoes were 65 cents, and that's all they cost. But I didn't have the 65 cents ... Dad didn't have 65 cents. So, Buster Wright down there was thrashing, and he hired me to help thrash and just exactly when he paid me that evening, just a co-incidence—I had earned 65 cents for helping him thrash, and that's exactly what my gym shoes cost. So, see, I couldn't take my money out here and spend it for pop and candy. It had to go right back in to buy myself something. A lot of kids, if they worked out here for a farmer, they'd take their money, and they'd go spend it on candy and pop. I wasn't allowed to do that. If I made a quarter some place, I probably, when I got home, would have to go to the store and buy a couple pounds of sugar.

HUGH: You would work on the railroad.

BOB: And kept Dad and Mom.

HUGH: You were a junior ... didn't you quit school once?

BOB: No, I didn't quit. One year when I was a junior in high school, I got a job on the railroad. I was 17 years old, and I worked all summer. When school time came in September, I said, "I'm not going back to school, I've got a good job. I'm making $5.28 a day." So, I worked and worked up till November. I decided to myself, "Well, Mom and Dad didn't give me any encouragement about going back to school." Because if you got a high school education back in those days, you were lucky.

HUGH: We weren't expecting that.

BOB: You weren't expecting it. You expected to go to the eighth grade and maybe drop out and that was it. Well, I decided I better get back to school. I sat down and wrote the principal, Mr. Corley, a letter to see what I could do. This was in November, right after Armistice Day. He wrote a letter back, and he said that if I would come back and take two subjects the rest of that first semester,

and make my back work up in those, and then in the second semester, I would take six solid subjects with no study halls, then I
could graduate with my class. That's exactly what I did. Then,
after high school was over, I went back and got a job at the railroad again. And then I knew that if I got my diploma, I could go
to college anytime I wanted to if I could ever afford to do so. So,
I worked on the railroad awhile, then went to the old Chevrolet
garage in Philippi, worked there a while. Then I went to Akron
and worked a while. I started to Broaddus in 1947 but didn't
have the money to continue. I only went for a week or so and
had to drop out because of finances. Then I ended up working
with the maintenance crew at the school building, and I decided
when I was working on these buildings (one time there were 72
school buildings in Barbour County). I decided when I was
working for the school board that if I can work on these buildings, I can work in them. If I ever get a chance to go to college, I
want to teach. And after that, I left the maintenance crew with
the school board, and I went to Southern States. I was assistant
manager at Southern States for a couple of years. I left there and
got a job driving a school bus in order to go to school. Drove a
school bus two weeks, and one evening, the transportation supervisor stopped me and said: "Bob, this is your last run this
evening."
I said: "Why?"
He said: "They turned you down in Charleston on your physical ex-
amination." There I was, without a job at the school board or
Southern States. Delma was pregnant with Debbie. So, I went
to Ohio and worked out there. I worked at Goodyear Aircraft. I
had an interest in this old store up here at Mt. Liberty with Russell. Russell got sick. He wrote me a letter and told me I'd have
to do something with the store. So, I worked out a notice and
came home and bought Russell's share of the store. I ran it for a
while. I bought Russell out, I ran the store for a while, and then
I sold the store.
One evening, Ben Green was driving the bus also. Now this was in

February, after I had left the school board in October, I believe, driving the bus. So, Ben Green stopped out at Mt. Liberty there and told me: "The transportation supervisor said there was a bus driver that quit, and that you've been off long enough, and you are eligible if you want to take another physical, and if you pass it, and your driver's test, the job is yours." So, I went down. The school board hired me. I took the physical. I took the driver's test, and I passed. Then I started to college.

I'd go to college, Alderson-Broaddus in Philippi, between bus runs, and drive to Fairmont on Wednesday nights through the summer. Finally, I got enough hours to teach in one-room schools, which was 64 hours, that was two years of college. I went out and taught three years, and I got a leave of absence from teaching, got a job driving the bus again, and I went back to finish school. In the meantime, I also worked at Philippi Hardware, too. I worked at Philippi Hardware part-time, drove the school bus, going to school, and trying to run the farm.

And Mr. Snyder, at the hardware store, didn't want me to teach. He wanted me to work full-time for him. He said: "I'll pay you as much as you are making teaching."

I said: "Well, it was a hard time and a long time getting this certificate. I think I better try it."

He said: "That will be fine, but anytime you get discouraged with teaching, you've got a job here."

So, I continued to work for him on Saturday and through the summer and Christmas vacations. One time during Christmas vacation, Mr. Snyder said: "Bob, how much do you make teaching?" Now this was about 10 to 12 years after I began teaching. He said: "How much are you making?" I told him. He said: "I can match that if you want to quit." And the day he found out I retired, I got a call from him to come in and work.

GARY: Never gave up, did he?

BOB: He never gave up! I went down, and I talked to him, and I said: "I can't work full time."

He said: "How about three days a week?"

"Well, that will be fine." Then I decided, "Nah, I'm getting old." So, I called him and I said: "Do I have to stick with that?"

He said: "No, Bob, you don't have to make that commitment if you don't want to. Maybe I shouldn't have even called you."

I said: "I'll tell you what I'll do. If you let me off under that commitment, anytime ever you need any extra help, you let me know."

He said: "That's good enough for me."

Then I went back to work for him part-time, even after that! But I never did go back full-time. It was a long, hard struggle.

GARY: Doesn't sound quite the way it is today, that parents pay the kids all the way through school and then sometimes we still have a hard time.

BOB: That's right. I know I have experienced this, being in school and working and paying your own way and seeing kids in there that have all kinds of money, and money sent to them, see, and there's a difference, quite a difference. I remember one time when I was principal at the Belington Junior High. I had a little trouble with a boy. He wasn't attending school very well. This is more or less a joke. I called him in the office and was talking with him. Well, he said: "Mr. Thompson, I really don't mind school too bad; it's just the principle of the thing." We started laughing together—the principal—"it's just the principle of the thing—oh! I didn't mean it that way!"

HUGH: Bob, do you remember how bow-legged William was? William was just about this high, and Marilyn Daughtery stayed with Mom when he was born, you see. She helped out when he was born. And Marilyn used to laugh. We had a little dog, her name was "Queen." She was about this high, and she was about this big around. William would be walking across the room to talk to Bob. We had a little wagon; Bob was in this wagon. And Marilyn said: "Absolutely now, I saw that dog run right between William's legs, and he didn't know nothing about it!" They said William was the most bow-legged kid that ever lived. Maybe he was a little heavy, when he started walkin', and his legs bowed out.

GARY: Bob, who was the biggest influence on you? I know a lot of our relatives, I think, were teachers. Going through the family tree, are several of them teachers?

BOB: Well, it's a little hard to make a decision, but there were several teachers that had an influence on me, and I … actually, when I was in about second or third grade, I thought I would like to be a teacher because—I'll tell you the reason why—because teachers were making good money at that time, whereas Dad was working on WPA for $35 a month, and teachers, some of them, were getting, now this was back in the thirties, some of them were getting $125 a month, you see. And that sort of influenced me. Teachers not only got paid good, because I have an old book back in the 1800s that said there were about five different certificates that you could receive, and they had different categories. I think the highest one was only $35 a month, but that was real good money back in the late 1800s and early 1900s. But I guess I'm not wanting to put out any particular teacher that had the most influence on me. But there was a lot of them that had an influence on me, and I know that I had some good teachers. Especially in my elementary schools. They were very concerned. I remember my teacher who gave us an award when we learned to count to 100. She would give us a pencil. Boy! I worked and worked hard. Finally, I made it! I'll never forget that pencil. Great big eraser on top of it. I'd see those pencils on her desk every day, and if another student got one, I thought: "I'll get mine tomorrow!"

I remember once when it was a very bad day, snowing and blowing. It was Valentine's Day. They weren't going to let me go to school because it was so bad. I had not missed a day all year, and I kept on and kept on, and Dad and Mom said I could go if William would go with me. So, William decided he didn't have school that day, that he'd go with me. So, we beat it out, and we walked up to Point Pleasant. William was the "Postmaster." We had the valentines in a big box, and he passed the valentines out. That evening, when we left the school, Louise Malcolm, now Louise Poling, at that time was the teacher. George and Jess Bennett, William, and I walked in front of Louise to break the road, so she could follow us. In time, the snow had that pass blown back over. When we got as far as Uncle Wade's, Louise said: "You boys are going over to the house, and you are going to warm before you start on home, and I'm going to open up something, some green beans." Louise opened up some green beans and said: "You boys are going to get something warm in your bodies before you leave here." So, she opened up some green beans and cooked them and we ate some warm food. Then we started. We got to the top of the hill there above where Tom Burner lives now, and we were three times at the top of the hill. The wind was blowing so bad, it would take our breath, and we would have to run back down and duck behind the bank again. The third time, we said: "We're going over this time." And we did!

And then, that same evening, June and Hugh had spent the same day with Roma Thompson, they had taken Roma to the doctor. They couldn't get in. They had to leave the car set in there some place, and they were afraid the battery would freeze up on it, so Hugh put the battery in an old feed sack and carried it home! But Louise Malcolm had a lot of influence on me when it came to teaching … and Delma had a lot of influence on me, because she was a teacher, too, you see, and she influenced me a lot of times.

GARY: Have any students that you considered kind of high points—that you felt like you influenced? I know you influenced a lot of them.

BOB: Oh yes! I do!

GARY: You influenced me, you taught me how to hit a ball. I got educated, too, but I remember that especially!

BOB: I've had some that failed, and I've had some that gone on to places … the thing of it is … some have been convicts, of course, that's society … I was very strict, but I was fair. I was firm, and I've had kids I put the paddle on meet me up there on the street, and they'd come up and shake hands with me and say: "Boy, I'm kinda glad you did that to me! You did me some good!" I didn't do it for mistreatment, I did it to try to correct them instead of trying to be an old meanie … I've had several of them that now I'm going to for advice! Jim Moore, remember him? He was at Valley Dell. Well, now he's the principal at Belington. There was something I was working on concerning math, and I went to Jim because Jim was a mathematician. He studied math, and I went to Jim for advice on how to work a problem, after I had taught him down there at Valley Dell how to multiply and subtract! But later, I had to go back to him for advice on working out a problem which was more complicated, things of this nature. And as I say, I went to school under Miss Louise Malcolm as a seventh and eighth grade student. Later, I became her principal. She taught under me at the Belington Junior High. So, this is how things worked out. But it was a hard row. If I had it to do over again, I guess I would do it again.

HUGH: I remember when you lived in Ohio and taught school out there.

BOB: Kenny Jacobs, John Mitchell, Carol Mitchell and Delma … they were at the same school I was in Randolph, Ohio, 15 miles east of Akron, Ohio.

HUGH: I don't think you would remember when we were in school at Union, and I got in trouble with Roy Delaney. Now, the fourth grade, they were still in the little room? Well, anyway, Fox Marsh, I'll never forget him. He was up at the blackboard doing something, and I was sitting about four seats behind Roy Delaney. Roy Delaney didn't have no books. He said: "Hugh, how 'bout giving me your fourth grade geography?" Remember fourth grade geography, Bob?

I said: "Okay, here it is." And I slid it up the aisle to him.

He grabbed it. Fox Marsh turned around and he seen it.

He said: "Come here!" I got a whippin' every time I went to school!

He went in the cloak room, and he brought out a switch about like that, and he gave me one, I mean to tell you! I didn't cry, and I think that's what made him mad because I didn't cry. He said: "Just a minute." He wore that switch out, and he went in the cloak room and got another one, brought it out, and he really gave me one that time. I didn't cry though!

BOB: I remember at Point Pleasant school, Doris Griffith, Griffith at the time, now Murphy, was my teacher. I was in fourth grade. Carl Price was the principal. He taught the big room. And he liked to play softball. He would go to Shockey and Junior and all these places to play softball. When he would do that, he'd send the students he had left over into Doris' room. He'd send some fifth and sixth grade boys to stay with Doris, but he chose me out of the fourth grade, took me with him on his ball team. Now, buddy, if you think there weren't bad feelings there, between the boys in his room, when he'd select me, the only one, only one out of the little room that he would come over there and get, and that was me. Mr. Price ordered us all ball caps. The only time we used those ball caps was when we were on a game. So, we went to Shockey one day to play a ball game, we had those little caps on. He measured our heads, and you had your own individual caps, but he took care of it. So, we went to Shockey to play a ball game down there and it started raining and those ball caps faded! … All those different colors! … Boy! I'll never forget that! I remember another thing about that year, too. Carl only taught up there one year, but I remember how many ball games we played and how many we lost. We played 11 games and we only lost two!

GARY: Now, what year was that?

BOB: 1936.

GARY: And that year you were still at Point Pleasant?

BOB: And we played Shockey, down on 92. We played Junior. We played Corley. We went to Belington to their grade school, and they had all kinds of kids to select from. See, they would have a whole room full of eighth graders, you know what I mean? And we would beat them! We went across the hill, over to what is Industrial Park now. There was a ball diamond up in there … there was a big board fence all around that diamond. The high school played their football games over there, too. Hugh, surely you remember that. I know how you remember it, too … Philippi was playing Belington in a football game one time, and you were working at the woolen mill, and Bud Jones was with us, and Linda, Bill Mitchell's wife … Linda Smith, Rose Finley. Bud Jones, and myself and Homer Poling.

HUGH: Homer Poling, yeah … he's dead now.

BOB: And you didn't go to work that night, you had Homer check you in! I remember that very well. Homer said: "You don't want to go to work tonight? Hugh, you don't have to, I'll check you in!"

HUGH: Did I have that '35 Ford?

BOB: You had that '37 Ford, I believe.

HUGH: Oh, okay.

BOB: I believe that's the one you had. I remember going over to that football game.

HUGH: William was going to come up. I loaned him the 1937 Ford, and he wrecked it! He flipped it on it's top. Milton White was with him. Also, they had just picked up Joey Farley. He was hitch-hiking. William came in and said: "I wrecked your car." I said: "Is it hurt?" He said: "Oh, not too much." I went up there, and I couldn't get it out! I had to take a bumper jack and jack the top up, so I could get in it and start it up. It turned right over on it's top. I turned it over. Raymond Fridley was the one who helped me turn it over, and he said: "Hugh, you better check the oil." It had been laying on its top for what, a couple of hours. I put a couple of quarts of oil in it and drove it home.

BOB: You may have gone to work later that night. I don't remember. Homer was still in high school. He was working after school hours, Homer Poling was, at the woolen mill.

HUGH: Were you working there?

BOB: I didn't work there. William did.

HUGH: Oh, William did.

GARY: I guess all you Thompson's were pretty famous for ball playing. What do you remember playing ball? I know me and Tommy and Chuckie ... I got a letter from Tommy not too long ago, and he was telling me some of the things he really remembered was when they'd come in, Grandma would make a ball out of socks, she'd sew it with thread. We'd bat that thing around out there in that little yard with a broomstick. Now, did you guys start the same way?

BOB: Yes, indeed! That's exactly the way we started.

HUGH: We had to make our own ball.

BOB: I played ball. I expect it was first or second grade.

GARY: Now, you played in, basically, almost in what would be the minor leagues around here? Or what kind of leagues did they have?

BOB: The Mountain State League was the last team I played with. Belington, with the Mountain State League. It was classified as semi-pro ball ... The reason that I know that is because that year there was a book that came out. It was put out by the National Baseball of Congress, and it had Belington's name in there ... and I'd love to get ahold of that book. I don't know where to see about it. I've asked Fred Holmes if he knew anything about Charles' belongings because Charles Holmes, Fred's dad, was our manager there one year, and I'm pretty sure he had one of them. And Bill, Bill Jones had one ... he was one of our commissioners, and I just wish I knew. Fred Holmes said he didn't know anything about any of Charles' belongings. But I thought maybe if I might look in the library up in Elkins, or someplace ... oh, there's a way of finding out, but I'm pretty sure it would recognize the league. The National Baseball of Congress classified us as semi, probably Class D or something like that. It wouldn't have been a Triple A or anything of that nature. When you go into Triple A, you go in the big league, don't you?

GARY: Yeah.

HUGH: I remember one time we had a ball game. I didn't practice or nothing. Ed England bawled me out one night. He said: "You little son of a gun, you don't come to practice, you ain't gonna play!"

So, I said: "Okay." So, I went down there. I was going with Mary Jones, way down there. She lived near the Corley schoolhouse. One day, about 1:00 on a Sunday, I said: "Mary, how about walking up to Mt. Liberty with us? We're going to have a ball game up there."

"Well, okay."

We went up there and I was standing behind the backstop, see, and Ben Green came up to bat. There were three guys on base. You remember that? And Ben Marsh over there was pitching. So, Ed said: "Hold it up, hold it up. I'm going to put a pinch hitter in." He put me in there, and the second ball that came over was high, and I loved them high balls! And I hit a home run and won the ball game! You remember that Bob?

BOB: I don't know whether I was there or not.

HUGH: I knocked it clear over that fence out there.

BOB: When we played with the Mountain State League, one Sunday I pitched Elkins out 11 to nothing. We went to the prison farm up at Huttonsville the next Sunday and played the prisoners. They had a runner on first base. Just as I was getting ready to make my delivery, I heard the coach tell the runner, he says: "Now when the pitcher throws that ball, you steal second." That runner looked around and said: "Man, what do you think I'm in here for?" Come to find out he was in there for stealing!

GARY: He wasn't going to do it again, huh?

BOB: He'd never do it again! I was laughing so hard I had to come to a stop. It's a wonder the umpire hadn't called "ball" on me, but he didn't.

HUGH: Oh, boy, those were the good old days, weren't they? I went up there to Huttonsville one time. I was in a farm training program. That was the first time we had ever seen a potato digger. They'd go along and the potatoes would come up. They had different size holes, and the little ones would drop in and the big ones would come up to the top.

July 9, 1994 - Hugh and Gary Thompson continue:

GARY: I wanted to find out where you were in the Army. You got drafted, or volunteered? I can't remember.

HUGH: I got drafted.

GARY: So, where did they send you first?

HUGH: They sent me to Fort Hayes, Ohio. I went from Fort Hayes, Ohio, to Camp Gruber, Oklahoma.

GARY: Okay, and from Camp Gruber … well, which one was basic training?

HUGH: Basic training was in Camp Gruber, Oklahoma. There's where I had to learn to march. Then we went from there. I was there about … I only had about six months training. We went from there to Camp Polk Louisiana. We went through … underneath machine gun fire and all like that. This one guy said: "Hey! I don't think them are real bullets." So, he stuck his steel helmet up. He took his steel helmet off. They called him "Alligator." You crawled under that, didn't you?

GARY: Yep.

HUGH: So, binnnnng! … He said: "That's live ammo!"

So then, they told us, our Colonel, Colonel Hawkins said: "Now save your money. You might see the bright lights."

Well, we knew for a fact that we were going to New York to get on a boat. We didn't know it for sure. We went up pretty close to New York. He said: "Don't pitch no puppy tents because we are headed overseas. I promised you to see the bright lights. Can you see them?" Yeah, we could see them from a long distance. But we thought we were going to get to go to New York and see the bright lights before we would get on the boat. So, he said: "No use to pitch the puppy tents, sit on your barracks bags."

Well, I had a barracks bag and a sea bag packed, and we went from there over to New York, went up the gangplank to get on a boat. They said: "Don't give your first name or anything. If they say your first name, just say Thompson. Okay. We sat on our barracks bags all night that night before we moved out on that ship. Then we needed a canteen of water. You couldn't go from here to that tractor. That boat, the MONTEREY … by the way, that guy that was over here yesterday, he was on the MONTEREY once. So, we got up there, and we would line up to go get a canteen full of water. Then we'd line up and we would get up on the top deck. I was on the bottom deck to start with. It took three days to get up to the top. And we had it, when we pulled out of New York harbor, it took us 45 minutes, pretty close to an hour, for everyone to get on the top deck to jump overboard in case we had to. Do you know how much we done that? We trained on the way out of New York harbor. In about three days, we could do it all. We could take everyone off that ship in 15 minutes. First, we started lining up in columns of two, going up the steps, then we done it with three, then with four, and everyone knew just exactly what to do and at what time. You heard a little whistle. We got that down so pat everyone could have got off that boat in 15 minutes. Seven thousand people. It was built for 600. There was 7,000 soldiers on it, mind you, not even counting the crew, the guys that fed us and cooked, and the guys that ran it.

GARY: What was the name of the boat?

HUGH: The MONTEREY.

GARY: The MONTEREY. And that went from New York to where?

HUGH: We went to Oran, Africa. And we stopped there for about two weeks. I'll never forget this. I was a Corporal, and Sargent Smith, he was a 1st Sargent. Well, we got liberty to go to Casablanca. And the 1st Sargent took a truck and took us all down there. He got drunk and wrecked the truck. Well, they fired him …

GARY: Broke him?

HUGH: Broke him. Then Mike Salaski, or something like that, he was from Milwaukee, Wisconsin, he took over. He was a great guy. He used to be a wrestler. He said: "Now let me tell you something. This wrestling is not real. One time I was supposed to win, and in the next town I was supposed to lose. I forgot and won. That messed the whole thing up!" Boy! He weighed about 250, all muscle. I'll never forget that guy. And he took over as our 1st Sargent.

And Sargent Smith, he's the one that got busted. He was the 1st Sargent to start with, but he got busted on account of wreckin' that truck going into Casablanca. So, one day we were out there and here comes the shells in, and the bombs. Old Sargent Smith, the last thing I seen of him, he dived under this haystack. Well, a big piece of shrapnel about that big around hit him in the rear. "Oh, my God! I'm dead! I'm dead!"

Well, I jumped right in behind him, and I said: "Take it easy, take it easy." I said: "You know, when you used to be 1st Sargent, you used to give me a hard time."

He said: "Yeah, I did, didn't I?"

I said: "Now, I'm a Corporal, and you're a Private. Now I'm going to give you a hard time!"

"No, don't do it. . ." he said.

I said: "Oh, okay!" We had a little fun ... sometimes I think about it and sometimes I'd like to forget it. But we had fun along the way.

GARY: So, you stopped in Oran, Africa for two weeks, then where did you go from there?

HUGH: We went from Oran to Naples Harbor. Algiers? Was it Naples? No, we went to Algiers first.

GARY: You went to Algiers first, is that still in Africa?

HUGH: Now I forget! Anyway, I think we went from Casablanca, or North Africa, Oran. You know what? We got off the boat in Oran. We would throw cigarettes over to all these kids waiting for them. And it was the dirtiest harbor you have ever seen in your life. You could see "rass-a-foo" floating around on the water. Those kids would dive in there when we would light a cigarette and throw it over in the water. They'd get it, and buddy, they'd smoke it. So Old Smith, he'd take a cigarette and dob two or three little pieces of grains of powder back in there, light it and throw it in the water. A kid would pick it up! Oh, boy! He started smoking, and it would blow up! Oh, man, it scared the heck out of him! You can imagine.

We left there and we went to, by heck, I don't know! Algiers? No, I believe we went to Naples Harbor. Anyway, they had just took Naples, the United States did. The 88th Infantry and the 34th Infantry ... and they bombed when we were there. Well, we had just got off the boat and were walking around what you call the college place. Big college. Well, we slept on the ground, and we seen all these lights and stuff, flares, and bombs. And they just bombed that ... well, anyway, we started running, and our Colonel said: "Hit the ground! Hit the ground!" Well, if you lay down, and something comes in, it explodes and goes up like that—250 yards. So, we hit the ground, and I told Smith: "Hey! Just like the 4th of July!" 'Bout that time one came in pretty close to us! "No, this ain't the 4th of July!" Boy! I hugged the ground that night! We had activity all night.

GARY: That was Naples?

HUGH: Uh, huh, Naples. So, we looked around, and we seen these bombers coming. The Germans were bombing Naples, and they bombed that ... what's that big ... Pompeii. You know where Pompeii was and all that: Mt. Vesuvius had lava coming down. They were trying to hit that. They figured lava would flow down on us and that would put us out of commission, but they missed us. We looked around and here's a couple of bombs hit the back of our ship, the one we just got off of. It just took the whole back end off. Now that was a big boat. We went from New York to Africa on that MONTEREY, but we got on another boat some way or another. It was a little old boat. But they hit it, right after we got off of it.

GARY: What company were you in? Were you in the same company or same division the whole time? The same one you went through basic training and all that with? What was the company?

HUGH: 985th Artillery. And Thomas Moore down there, he was

in the 173rd, and there was a Myers down here, we were always kind of pretty close together. I'd see them.

GARY: That was the division? How many men were in a division?

HUGH: About 8,000.

GARY: So, you were in a certain company then, too?

HUGH: Yeah, I was in the 985th Field Artillery.

GARY: 985th Field Artillery. How many men were in that? The 985th.

HUGH: Well, let's see. We had A Battery, B Battery, C Battery, F Battery ... I don't know, we had about five batteries.

GARY: Which battery were you in?

HUGH: Service Battery.

GARY: You were in the Service Battery?

HUGH: I had to fix the guns when they would quit firing, and this and that. But I was on the road all the time. Them Germans had me zeroed in. They could tell when I left, those zero men. I had shrapnel go through my gas tank on the GMC truck. You had five gallons of gas on the side. One time, I had 128 holes in my truck.

GARY: What kind of truck did you drive?

HUGH: GMC. Six by six.

GARY: So, now—you fixed the guns ... you kept the guns firing. When the guns would break, you would ...

HUGH: I'd have to fix'em.

GARY: But then you drove truck when you were moving?

HUGH: Well, when I'd go from one battery to the other, to fix this gun here, and then maybe have to go up here and fix one. So, I was up at B Battery one time fixing one, and I was laying under this truck, and a big 210 came in ... is that right? A German shell. It lit within 30 feet of me. I'm telling you! That thing picked me up off the ground. It was a good thing I was under this truck. It picked me up off the ground and struck me two or three times up against the frame ... I looked over here, and I'll never forget his name, Captain Long. He said: "Tommy, are you hurt?"

I said: "No."

He said: "Well, I am."

I looked around and he had his left arm blew off ...

There was another time when it was the American planes shooting at us.

GARY: They were bombing their own guys and didn't know it?

HUGH: They shot holes all over my truck. The machine gun I had, you know on the truck, the machine gun goes round and round, it was on the turret of my truck. The machine gunner, his name was Logan ... we had a hell of a time finding him. He jumped off there and I said: "What good is that machine gun doing?" He was down underneath the truck!

Old Colonel Hawkins, he'd went ahead. He asked: "Tommy, what happened?"

I said: "I don't know." My windshield was shot out and everything. There was a bullet hole one inch from my foot. If I'd had a purple heart, I would have got out of the Army. I would have had five more points. I would have got out of the Army two months quicker. Oh, you don't understand this.

GARY: Oh, yeah, I do. Come over here and sit down. We're going to leave here in a few minutes. I'd like to find out more about where you were at over there.

HUGH: Well, I guess Cassino was the worst. I think it was the worst. It took four months to take that town.

GARY: From where you got off the ship, then what did they do? Did they just keep advancing after that? From Naples?

HUGH: Uh-huh. Yeah. Uh-huh.

GARY: Going north? Going up?

HUGH: Going up, up the boot. We were on the west side. Gearl was over on the other side, the east, over with General Montgomery. Gearl came up there and they wouldn't let him through. Three miles behind the front lines, he got a light. You can use your lights, from there on in you had to go blackout, you know what I mean? We were always about 200 yards behind the infantry. We supported the 88th Infantry. That Roberts boy down here was in the 88th.

GARY: So, now, what division was Gearl in?

HUGH: He was in the 21st Engineers, but he was way back from the front lines. The activity, action, that he had was airplanes bombing. Not even artillery. Artillery could shoot 22 miles accurate.

GARY: So how close were you to the front lines most of the time?

HUGH: About 250 yards. Always right behind.

GARY: Just right behind the Infantry?

HUGH: What do you call him came up there one time, one of the generals. "What are you doing up here? Fifty yards behind the infantry!" General Clark got bawled out because they put us too close to the infantry. By heck! I tell you something, those infantry guys would come back there. They would try to give them a rest once in a while. They'd come back there; they couldn't take it. They said: "No, I'd rather be up in front. I don't want to be back here with those bombs, those big old shells coming in here." They could kill you at 250 yards when one exploded.
And I'll never forget ... the Germans, they would pick us up. They'd watch the lights flash when the guns went off. They'd be up in the airplanes, see, little airplanes. Then they'd call in to their CP ... what's CP stand for? Oh, I forget ... anyway, they'd give them directions to shoot on us. So then, we started using flashless powder. You put a big shell in that piece, about as big as that. You put a 90-pound shell in, and put the charge behind it, nothing but black powder. Then you would shove the breech block, then you'd pull the lanyard, the rope to trip the trigger. You had to keep your mouth open, so it wouldn't burst your eardrums. The Germans were picking us up, see. They'd see the flash of those guns. Well, I've stood there on the front lines a lot of nights, 12:00 at night, pitch dark, and you could sit there and read a newspaper. And you would have to hold onto something, the ground would shake. Six hundred artillery pieces opened up all at one time. We took this hill ... well, Cassino was the worst. It took us four months to take that little town. They were so well fortified in there, the Germans. The Italians had already given up when we took Cassino, I'm pretty sure. But they were dirty.

They would be in a great big house, upstairs, looking down on us, and they'd radio and tell the Germans just exactly where our location was, and drop a shell in there. They started using smoke shells. They'd drop one in and then they'd say: "Well, you go on line, so many yards to the right, drop one. Now so many yards to the left, then so many yards to the front." And then they'd say: "Zero it in."… Them Germans would even shoot at one vehicle with artillery, a German 88. Purple Heart Valley. Boy! I'm telling you, that was something else. Purple Heart Valley, that's what it was called. Nothing but a valley, and the Germans there, and there, and everything. They'd fire on us all the time. Even if one vehicle went up that road, they'd fire on them with an 88. They had the 88. That was the best gun, according to everyone, that was ever made. The Germans made it. The Germans weren't no dummies, they were smart. So, then they had the guns back in the mountain. They'd pull them out on the railroad track and shoot. They'd even back up and you couldn't see them. Something like a pill box. You ever seen a pill box? Ever see any movies?

GARY: We watched *D-Day*. We watched the stuff about D-Day.

HUGH: I'll never forget D-Day … it was on my birthday. Me and Caruso, that little boy, little guy.

GARY: What was his whole name? Do you remember?

HUGH: Frank Caruso, C-A-R-U-S-O.

GARY: Where was he from?

HUGH: New Jersey, Brunswick … New Brunswick, and I never could get a hold of him.

GARY: New Brunswick?

HUGH: Uh-huh. And before he went in the Army, he was with about 15 other guys. They had motorcycles, Harley Davidsons. They'd go clear around the United States every year. He was something … So, him and I slept together. Someone asked me what a "sheltered half" was the other day. Sheltered half was half a tent; that's why they called it "half." You and your buddy pitched one little tent. He carried half of the tent, and I carried half. So, me and him started pitching a little tent together. On the sixth day of June, about 3:00 in the morning, I was standing guard. I had a 30/30 carbine, and I was leaning on an old fence rail. You know they had rail fences like this, and he was over there on the other point. I went over ... Well, we'd been fighting ... going for a long time, couldn't stay awake ... We was really wore out and tired. I shook him; had to wake him up. He fell asleep. Buddy, that's one thing you don't want to do—is fall asleep when you are fighting Germans. So, I shook him, and I said: "Hey! Caruso! They just made that big invasion!" We'd been hearing all about it, but we didn't know what it was going to be, and everyone said they made the invasion in the wrong place. There were a lot of men. I said: "They just made that big invasion. The war won't last very long now."

Well, it didn't. And it was my birthday ... hmmm.

GARY: Where were you at then? On D-Day?

HUGH: Still in Italy. We were up pretty close to Austria. I know a boy that got killed in Austria ... so we took that. Well, Cassino was the worst, then Bologna. We went by the Leaning Tower.

GARY: Leaning Tower of Pisa?

HUGH: Uh-huh ... I met Tom Poling up there. I was going up the street and he was going down. We met! I turned around. I stopped, turned around, and looked. He done the same thing. He said: "Wait a minute! Come here! Your name Thompson?"

I said: "Yeah, your name Poling?"

He said: "Yep!" First guy I ever seen, you know, from the United States which I knew from West Virginia ... old Tom Poling.

GARY: So, now, where were you when the war ended?

HUGH: Pretty close to Austria. And we were so happy! The captain said, Captain Beam, (I'll never forget him): "Now take your helmets out there, steel helmets, and paint'em. We're going to turn'em in when we get to headquarters." Well, I was paintin' mine. I had corporal stripes on them; you know, on top. 'Bout that time, shells started coming in! Well, me and Caruso got underneath this barn. Well, they quit shelling after a while.

Come to find out there was a panther outfit, German tanks, over there. We kept dropping leaflets in there—the airplane did—telling them the war was over. "No! It ain't over! We're going to win this war!" And they fought on us three days after the war was over. Now that's the honest God's truth.

GARY: Wouldn't quit, huh?

HUGH: Wouldn't quit! They couldn't believe that they had lost the war.

So, when we painted our helmets to make them look new, we took all the markings off the bumpers on the trucks and the tanks, and all that. Well, we thought we were going to get to go home. Well, I didn't have enough points 'cause I was only in the United States six months in the Army. Some of them, old National Guard outfits, had four or five hash marks. Been in there 15 years. Well, they had privileges over me. But anyway, we went back down there and came out with points to go home. Well, I had only 71 points. Had to have 75. So, after the war was over, I had to stay over there about four or five months to get enough points to come home. And I was over there in combat. A lot of guys never seen combat, but they had a lot of time in the Army. You were allowed so much for every year you'd been in. There wasn't nothin' fair about it ...

But I'll never forget there at Bologna. I had to go up this hill all the time to get gas for the battalion, and they'd fire on me going up there. They knew exactly when I was going out, the time, and the time when I'd get back. So, I got on top of the hill, and it was an old dirt road, you know. There was a donut stand there. American's put it up. Civilians! Two good-looking girls working this donut stand for the USO. I stopped there and got me some donuts, and I pulled away. I betcha I didn't get from here to across the road and the bombs came in there and killed them all. Them two girls, now they were volunteers. Just to help the soldiers out, you know. Giving us donuts and coffee ...

GARY: Who was the general that was in charge of your division?

HUGH: General Clark.

GARY: Clark?

HUGH: I think he's dead ... yeah.

GARY: Did he survive the war?

HUGH: Yeah.

GARY: Was he actually out there?

HUGH: No!

GARY: He was back behind the lines, a long ways?

HUGH: Oh, hell, yeah! I seen ... one time there was a couple more generals ... it wasn't Patton. He got killed. His jeep turned over. He got killed. He was "Old Blood and Guts." Oh, they gave him ... he lost a lot of men, but he ... I'm telling you, when he won, he won! You remember him. You probably heard enough about him. Old Patton. I seen him. He was back there with General Clark, and they didn't want to establish that beachhead. Anzio beachhead. Did you ever hear of that?

GARY: You weren't in Anzio, though, were you?

HUGH: I could hear them firing. I was here ... right here's Anzio beachhead, and we always went in a spearhead, like this. We was getting fire from here on the left side, the right side, and the front! Plus, airplanes dropping bombs. I don't know why we always went in a spearhead. They told General Clark: "Hey, that's wrong."

General Clark and all of them got bawled out for that. Roosevelt was the one that done it. Said: "Now let's take this beachhead right here, Anzio".

Why, hell! Up there in the mountain, the Germans were so well fortified. They'd have a pill box. They'd even have railroad tracks going back in the mountains ... they'd pull the big guns out and shoot and then pull'em in, so they couldn't get hit. And they told ... I'm tellin' you. I talked to some guy who was in the Navy. They wouldn't stay there. The Navy took all the soldiers in there and they let them get off, oh, I don't know, maybe say far as from here to the bottom of the hill, then they'd go in on ... what do you call them? Amphibians ... and get on land through the water. And the Germans started firing on them, and the Navy wanted to pull out! They pulled out! They wouldn't stay there. Deed, I'm telling you the truth, the Navy wouldn't stay there afterwards … They were damn glad to see all these soldiers get off their boats, so they could get the hell out of there. You better believe it … it's the truth.

GARY: Now, who was your next in command after General Clark?

HUGH: He was always my commander in the Army.

GARY: Now, then, who was under him? Did you have a …

HUGH: Colonel Hawkins. Yeah. You see you have generals, four stars, three stars, two stars. Then you got … well, General Clark, he was a two star … He wasn't a big, big shot, but he was over us. He was over the Fifth Army. Gearl, he was over on the other side of Italy, he was in the Eighth Army. Well, the Eighth Army was British … he was under General Montgomery.

GARY: Now, what did Gearl do? He was in the Engineers?

HUGH: He was in the 21st Engineers. All he done was deliver. He drove a big truck. He delivered dozers, and this and that, to different outfits. And I don't believe you could call him as being in combat lines. But I was in the front lines 22 months. I was only in the service 28 months. Six of it was in the United States. The rest of it was on the front lines.

GARY: So, when you started, you basically started from …

HUGH: Naples

GARY: From Naples all the way up …

HUGH: Kree'as … and that's in Italy.

GARY: Now, you had to stay there in Kree'as?

HUGH: On Route 7. I can take you there, and I can show you every place we were stalled. It took us months to take the little town of Cassino. Can you believe that?

You remember that big abbey on top of there? … The Germans had this big abbey, well, it belonged to the Italians. That's a religious joint. Oh, it was big … I bet it would reach from here to across the road, wouldn't it? And we were going to fire on it, but they wouldn't let us. Well, the Germans were using it for a CP, Command Post. And they would direct fire out of that building onto us and we got tired of it. That was Purple Heart Valley. We couldn't get the orders to fire on it. General Clark wouldn't let us fire on it. So, this one old guy, I'm telling you the truth, he got so peed off about it, he come on a shootin' that one gun by himself one night. He had it exactly right on that target and they caught him. They knocked him down and kept him from firing on it. Well, about a month later we got orders to fire on the Abbey and destroy it. We leveled it. It was bombed.

I tell you one thing, I'd sure like to get hold of some of those guys I fought with, even if they are dead, I'd like to get hold of their families. I'll never forget them. Most of them were from Milwaukee and Green Bay, Wisconsin. It's hard to remember their first names because we never went by first names. It was just like my name is Thompson, but they called me "Tommy," short for Thompson.

GARY: Maybe some of those battles were filmed. Photographers were there, there should be pictures or movies, maybe we could find some of that stuff.

HUGH: Oh, yeah, they used to take movies. I was hoping I would someday get to see one. We had just took this hill. It was raining. It rained for 40 days and 40 nights one time. You might not believe that, but it did. We were going up there, and I picked me up a little dog about this long and that high, a black and white dog. It took it out of its nest from its mother, and I took it with me. And my 1st Sergeant said: "You can't keep that dog. You can't keep it." I said: "You wait and see. I'll hide it."

Every time the inspection guy came around, I'd hide it under my seat. We were going up this mountain. I had that little dog, see. No windshields, it was covered up with canvas. I had this little dog sitting up there. He always wanted to sit up there when I was driving. I looked up, and here was some guy up there with a movie camera. I always thought I would like to see that. It's there somewhere, but I don't know where a guy would ever see it.

GARY: I'm not sure.

HUGH: I thought maybe they might have put it on a newsreel someday, you know.

GARY: Oh, it probably was. If a person just knew when they were going to show it.

HUGH: I wrote Mom a letter and told her about it. She watched all the news, and she never did see it.

But the funny thing about the Anzio beachhead. They said you could stand around and count the old men, the rest of them were killed. You ought to go there. I'll take you over there some of these days, Anzio beachhead. I've been there. They have a big graveyard. It's kind of hard to understand—why did they do that? They said you can stand around and count your old men at 12:00 at night. They said if the Germans had kept firing two more hours, there wouldn't have been no Anzio beachhead. But they just coincidentally quit firing, and they rushed in. Then they started getting replacements, replacements.

GARY: Okay, so let's talk now about what you did after the war. So, when did you get married? Before or after the war?

HUGH: After the war, after I came back.

GARY: So where did you meet Mom at?

HUGH: Oh. It was before I went into the service, in 1941 or '42.

GARY: So how did you meet her?

HUGH: Well, I was in Washington, DC, working as a mechanic, out there in a car lot. So, I would come in here, and my mother wrote me a letter and said: "Hugh, you just as well come in. Gearl's working down at the woolen mill. He got his call to the Army." Well, before I came in, he got his call. So, I thought: "By heck, I'd better go, because Gearl went, I'll be the next one." And my mother told me in a letter, "You'll be the next one called out of Barbour County."

Well, I came in here and I had a '35 Ford, a four-door sedan. So, William told me: "Hey, there are some good-looking Corley girls moved from Junior down to Union." He knew I was interested; you know.

So, I said: "Are they going to school down there?" They were going to the high school.

Okay, so I go down there with William, and I'm going down into the basement, you know, where the furnace used to be. Did you ever go to the old high school down there? So, I started down them steps, and William says: "There's one ... Mavis!" And I started talking to her. From then on, I would always drive down there. I knew exactly when she would get on the school bus to come home. I would park there in front of the schoolhouse and every time I seen her get on the bus, she would always get in the back end, so she could wave at me. Tantalize me! So, I would follow her home very neared every night, and she would wave out the back of the bus.

GARY: Now, when was that? 1941?

HUGH: 1941 or '42. Because I went in the Army, let's see — it was December 21st. Inducted, I mean. I was a soldier.

They said: "Now, we're going to treat you pretty good. We're going to let you go back home and spend Christmas and be back here on the 27th of December." Over to that big motel over in Clarksburg. I forget the name of it. (Stonewall Jackson Hotel) Anyway, we got to come home for Christmas and when we went back, we went from Clarksburg to Fort Hays, Ohio. Got all our uniforms, clothes. Funny thing, going through that line, they said: "What size shoes do you wear?"

I said: "Seven-and-a-half."

"Okay." They gave me size twelves!

I said: "Them are too big!"

"Hey! You keep your damn mouth shut! You get through there! You're in the Army now!" Boy, when I got up to Camp Gruber, Oklahoma, my pants were three sizes bigger. Everything I had was, and here were my No. 12 shoes settin' down there. So, I talked with my 1st Sergeant. I said: "Hey! I can't wear them."

He said: "I don't blame you." I come in and got shoes that fit me. When I was overseas, you always carried one extra pair of shoes on you. Well, I would wear one pair and save the new ones, you know, for this Māori. He was fighting with us.

We had these British ... right down below us ... Māori ... they were from India ... I forget. Anyway, he wanted those shoes. I had them in my barracks pack. I said: "No, I can't do that. I have to have an old pair to turn into RIA." If you got an old pair to turn in, you can get a new pair. He gave me a German luger for it, a brand-new gun, loaded. It's a pistol, a revolver. And I couldn't resist that, so I found an old pair of shoes. I turned them in and got my new pair. Oh, heck, I'll tell you something—in Africa, you know what they would do? The French Moroccans? They would come around and they would dig up dead American soldiers. You don't believe that do you ...?"

GARY: What year did you get out of school? What was the last year you went? You started off, you went to Point Pleasant, right? You went to school at Point Pleasant first. Was that the first school you went to?

HUGH: I think ... maybe it was Valley Dell, no ... Mt. Liberty. Then Valley Dell, then Point Pleasant. Then I started to high school in 1940 ... 1941. Anyway, I finished my first year and then my second year. I always fell down in mathematics, civics, and science, but I took that manual training. In Vo-Ag, I would make such a high grade that it brought my average up. You see, they averaged it, and that's the only reason I passed.

So, one day, I forget who was with me, but we asked Mr. Woodford ... Was Woodford ever your teacher? Someone said he's still living in Buchanan. Well, anyway, we went in there and asked him—it was on a Friday—if we could go to the Forest Festival. "Nope!"

So, I said: "Well, we're going anyway!" And we did.

We went back to school on Monday morning, and I was expelled for the rest of the week. They expelled me for three or four days. I finally got back. Then the last time, I said: "To hell with you, I'm going to Washington, DC." So, I went over there to Poling's Store, where Poling's Store is now, stuck my thumb out and started thumbin'. I was going to Washington, DC, to get me a job, and that's what happened.

GARY: So how long did you work in Washington, DC? You were a mechanic out there?

HUGH: Yeah, I was there about ... from the last part of '39 ... I believe ... no, the last part of '40 or '41, and most of '42 because I came in in December, around Christmas in '42.

GARY: What was the name of the place you worked out there?

HUGH: Shepherd Park Motor Sales ... yeah, and I got Herbert a job. I got him over there. And I got Ralph Poling, who runs Poling's Store over there, a job. About as far as from here to that house over there, in the White Coffee Pot. That's a little restaurant, they had white coffee pots. But anyway, he stayed with me. I got my room first, you see. I had two rooms near Rock Creek Park. And I got June out there. Well, he became head mechanic, over top of me. And Madge and little Shirley. So, we got Ralph to come out. He stayed with us. He gave June something. After June came out there, I turned all the apartment rings over to him, and he would charge us all $12 apiece for rent, and that was feeding us too. So, Ralph, me, and another guy.

GARY: So, what year did you come back? When you went into the Army? In 1942?

HUGH: I left Washington, DC, in 1942 to go to the Army.

GARY: 1942. Then when did you get out of the Army?

HUGH: 1945.

GARY: 1945. What did you do right after that? Did the Army send you to any kind of schools?

HUGH: Well, I went to diesel mechanic school at Camp Gruber, Oklahoma, to be a diesel mechanic.

GARY: In the Army?

HUGH: Yeah.

GARY: And after you got out of the Army, where did you go and what did you do?

HUGH: I came home, like a dummy, and married Mavis!

GARY: Well, she waved at you from the school bus all the time, right? Did she write to you while you were over there?

HUGH: Yeah, and I'd write her. V-Mail, you know, it would go by air. Little old fine writing. So, I got out, I believe it was about the same time I went in, only in 1945. 23rd or 24th of December in 1945. No! Wait a minute, I got that wrong … November I got out, 22nd or 23rd—sometime around there. And on the 19th of December, me and Mavis got married. That's the 19th, because I remember I wanted to do it on account of William's birthday; he was born on the 19th of December.

GARY: So, where did you get married at?

HUGH: Philippi.

GARY: Where at in Philippi?

HUGH: I can show you the old house. Right in behind, you know where the South End Market used to be on this end? … If you were going down by Grab-a-Nickel and go out there, pass the South End Market, you come out on Main Street. It was right back in there. It's the Philippian Chapel now.
The preacher's name was Burnett.

GARY: So, it was in his house?

HUGH: We had to take a blood test and all like that. We went in there, and he married us. Herbert was with us. Herbert and Carol were already married.

GARY: So, Herbert and Carol were the witnesses?

HUGH: Yeah, so they went with us to get married, and I'm telling you, that night it snowed so bad. I had a '35 Ford, no, I had a '37 Ford. We went up this hill, and I said: "I can't get down that hill." I started down, and I started slidin'. I cut the wheel, but it didn't make no difference. It went clear up on the sidewalk and clear through a man's yard and back down.
Then we decided we'd go eat. At that time, they called it the City Restaurant, beside the movie theater. There's an ice cream shop there now. Herbert and Carol wanted to make sure they were going to get us our wedding supper. Well, we went in there and he ordered up steak. Boy! We had a big supper!

GARY: So, then Janet was born a year later?

HUGH: Ten months after we were married, Janet came along.

GARY: Where did you work after you got married?

HUGH: Shorty Haddix'—No, me and June ran a shop down there.

We made good money down at Gordon Knapp's Then some way or another, Shorty Haddix told me he would like for me to come down there. And I said: "Well, we're doing pretty good up here." But he said: "No, I want you to come down and work with me." So, I went down there. At that time, if you had just got out of the Army, you had the right to sign up and get you some tools. Well, I went to work with Shorty Haddix.

Photo by Donnie Thompson Photography

ACKNOWLEDGMENT

I was married for 52 years to a wonderful companion, Basil. He passed away suddenly on November 1, 2017. A day has yet to pass without my thinking of him and our life together. Most of my writings were done before he died, making him an integral part of my experiences which have contributed to this book.

In October 2020, I composed a poem on coping with the death of your spouse.

BASIL DELANEY
1947 – 2017
Loved Husband, Father and Friend

Jesus said ... "The one who exercises faith in me,
even though he dies, will come to life." John 11:25

All interior graphics prepared for publication by Jodi Delaney-Yates

Why Are You Still Here?

Why are you still here?
Losing you was so unexpected.
But it was real. I was there.
This is not about denial or grief.
This is about your constantly walking
Through my mind, without my permission.
    I need to proceed to live without you.
You are gone, but I am here.
I am okay; I still see rainbows and sunsets.
I wake up, do what I do, and I go to sleep.
I am living, I enjoy the blessings I receive.
But why are you still here?
    Why does everything I see and hear
Bring back a memory of you and of us?
A man will leave his father and mother and
Stick to his wife, and they will be one flesh.
When you died, I became one flesh,
Single, I am here alone. You are not here.
    I have studied God's Word.
I know the dead are alive in his memory.
I know He will have a yearning for you.
He will call you. You will wake up,
Along with my other loved ones,
And then, you will be here.